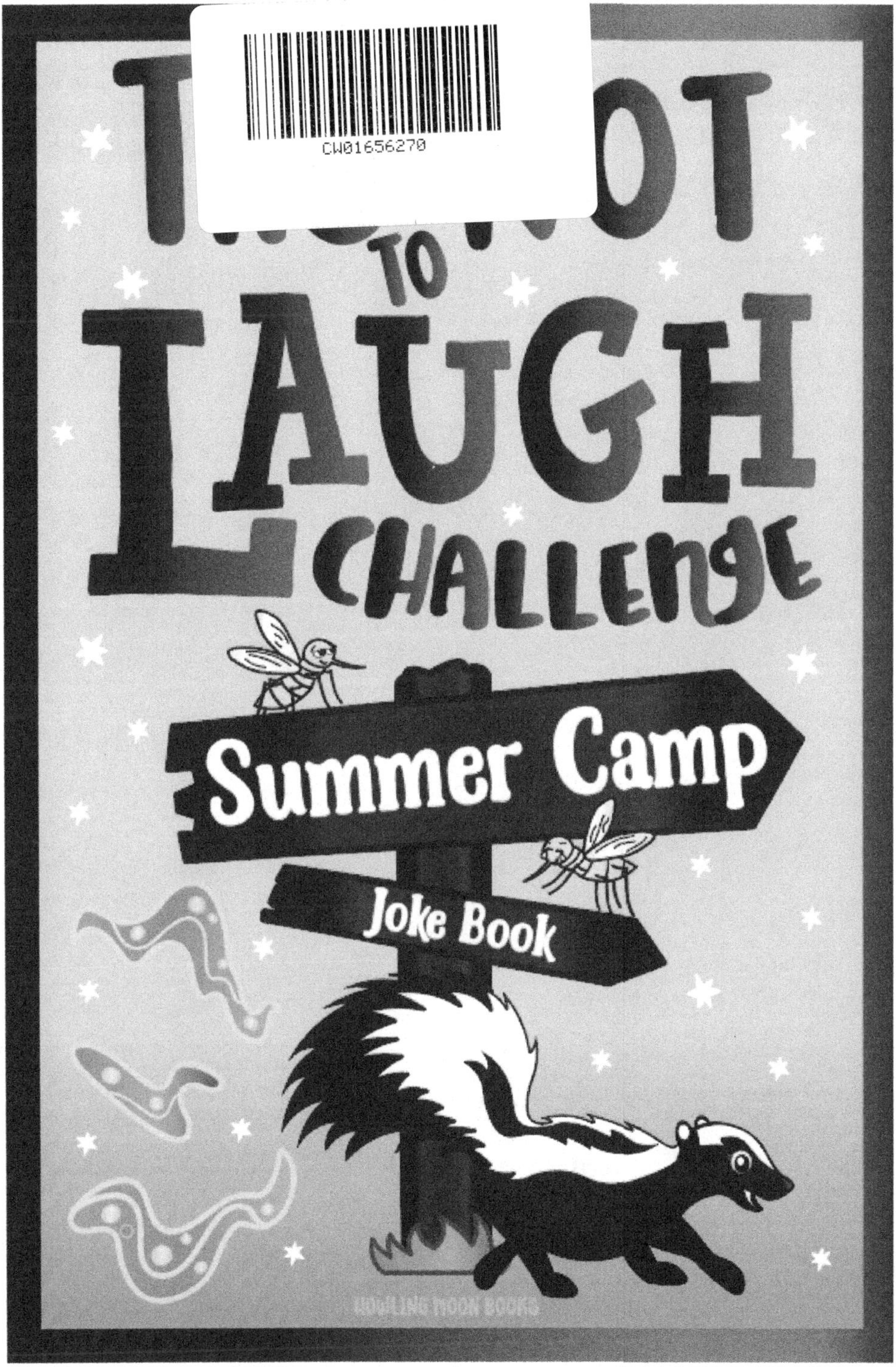
TO
LAUGH
CHALLENGE
Summer Camp
Joke Book
HOWLING MOON BOOKS

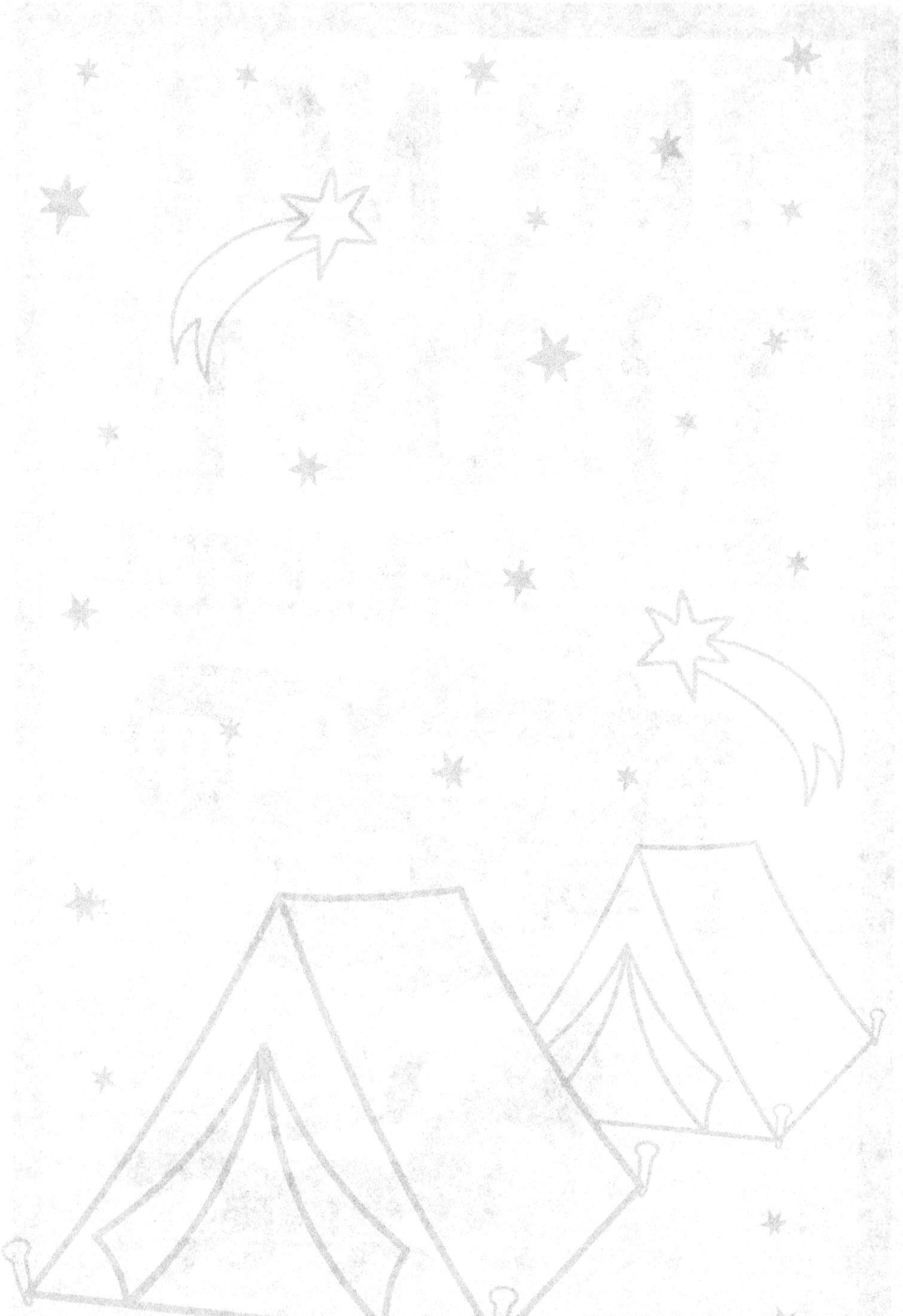

HOWLING
MOON BOOKS

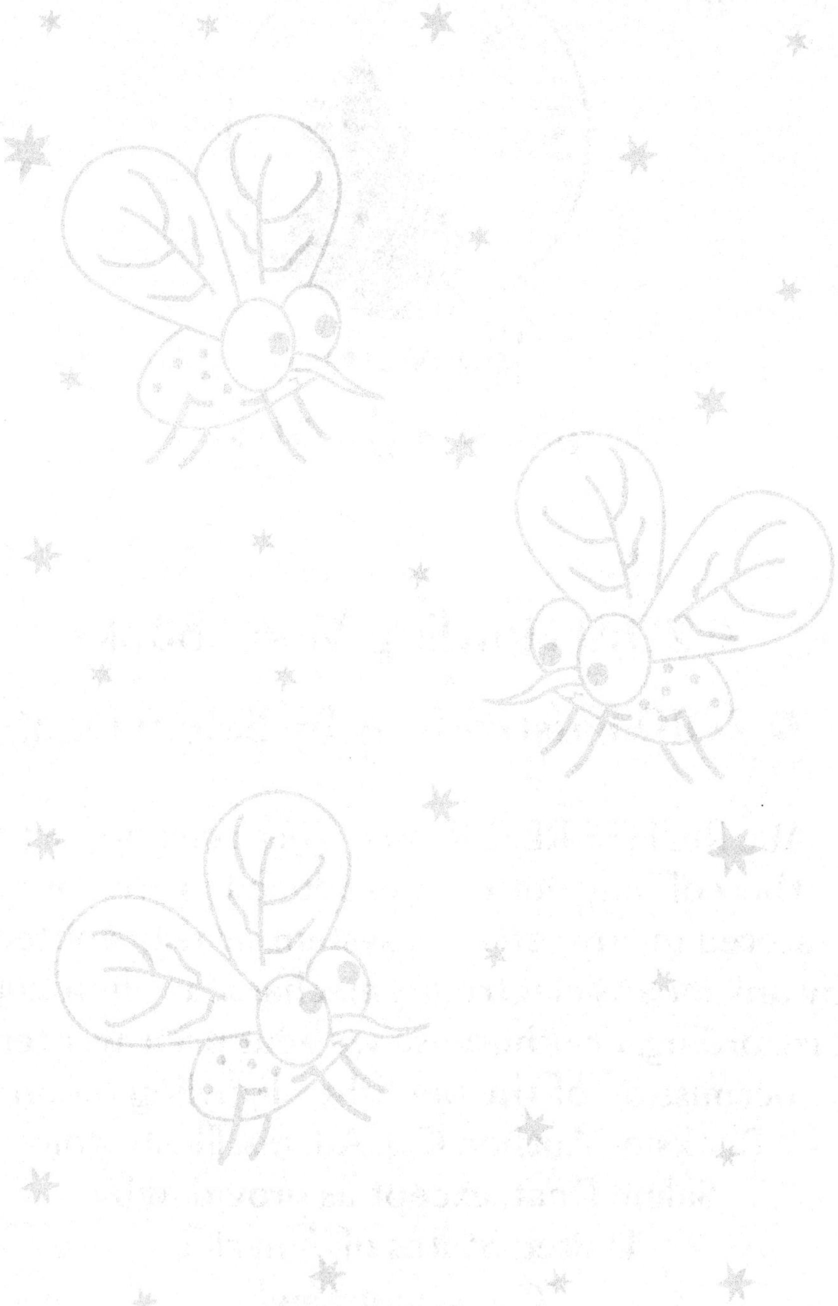

Spread S'more Laughter
with these Brand-New, LOL,
Campsite-Approved Jokes
that Family & Friends
will Enjoy!

You can choose to play the popular
Try Not to Laugh Challenge Game
OR
you can read the book for lots
of campfire giggles!

Please consider leaving us a review
on Amazon.com. We value your
feedback & greatly appreciate
your time!

Happy Camping!

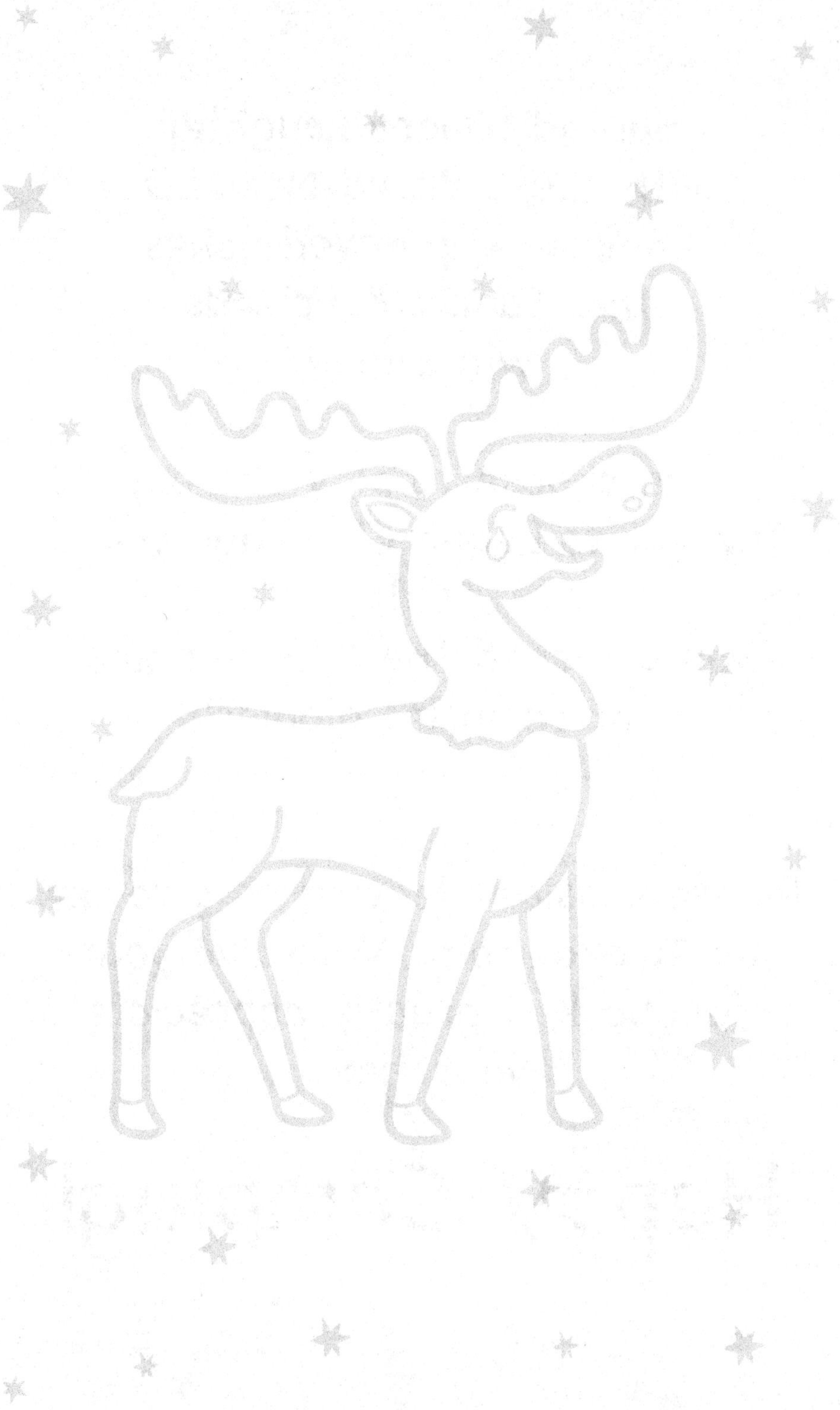

What are moose afraid of?

Moose-quitos!

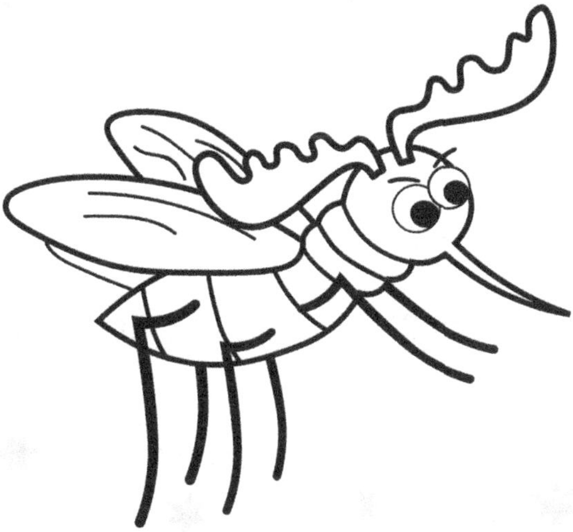

What is a canoe's favorite drink?

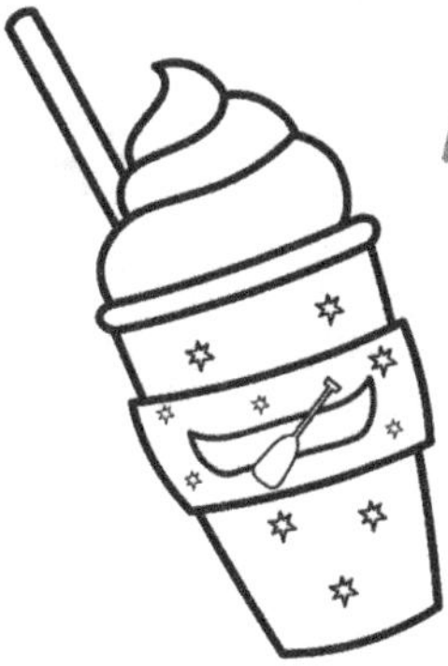

An ice cream float!

What do you call a broken compass?

Lost!

Why can't you sneak up on binoculars?

They can see you coming a mile away!

How do eagles catch so many fish?

They are very talon-ted!

What phrase are earthworms frightened of?

The early bird gets the worm!

What is the best advise you can give an earthworm?

Sleep in late!

Why was the volcano feeling sick?

It wasn't feeling so hot!

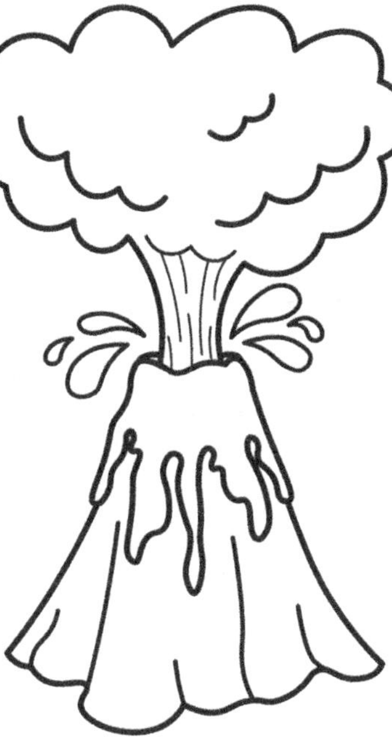

What is a frog's favorite drink?

Hot Croak-o!

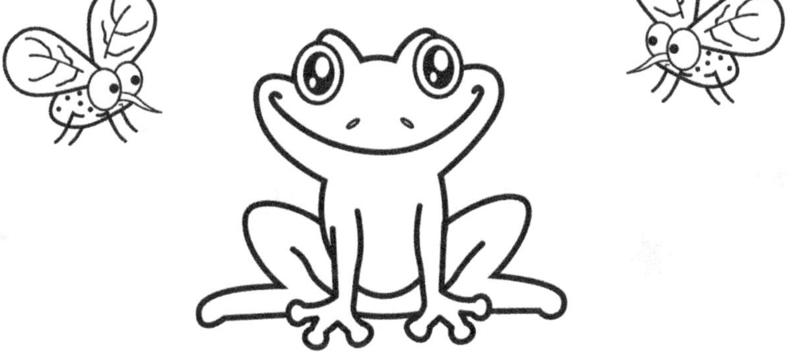

What did the donuts think about summer camp?

They liked the hole thing!

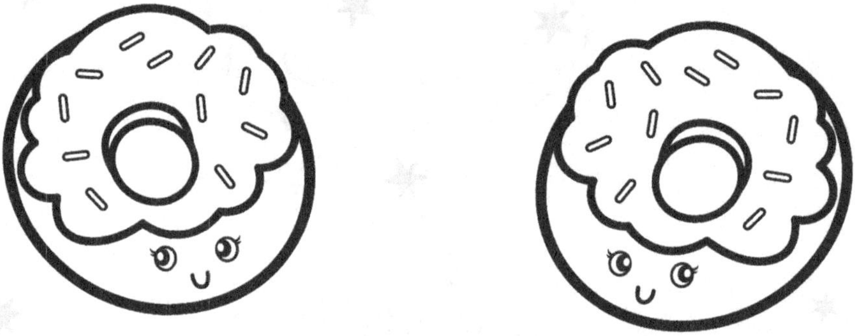

How did you measure poison ivy?

By the itches!

Why do fish like to eat worms?

Because they get hooked on them!

What do you call a boy who wears jeans on his camping trip?

Levi!

What do you say to campers before they zip line down the mountain?

It's all downhill from here!

Why are campers down to earth?

Gravity!

What is the difference between a fly & a camp lunch?

One's hard to shoo & the other is hard to chew!

The slug family couldn't believe their camping week was over!

How slime flies!

Why couldn't the snake talk?

He had a frog in his throat!

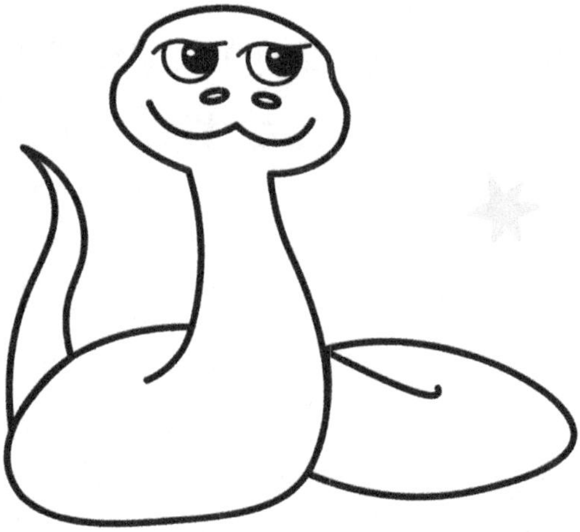

What did the fishing pole say to the fish?

This is the end of the line for you!

Where do grizzlies stay on vacation?

In a bear bnb!

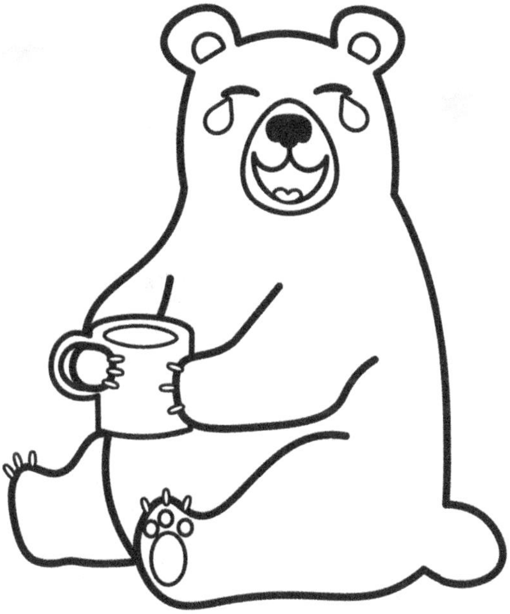

What flowers are wimpy?

Pansies!

Why was the river so annoying?

It had a big mouth!

Where do campers tell the most ghost stories?

At Jam-BOO-rees!

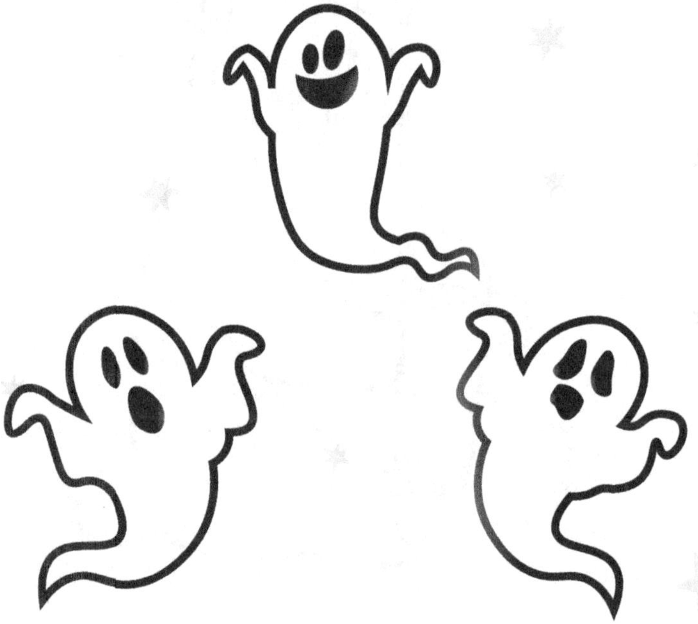

What kind of books do rock climbers read?

Cliffhangers!

What is a camper's motto?

Campers are s'more fun!

Why did the campers sing softly around the campfire?

Because the tent was full of sleeping bags!

What should you do for someone who goes to fishing camp?

Drop them a line!

Why did the little star go to the bathroom?

He had to twinkle!

What do you call a baby skunk?

A little stinker!

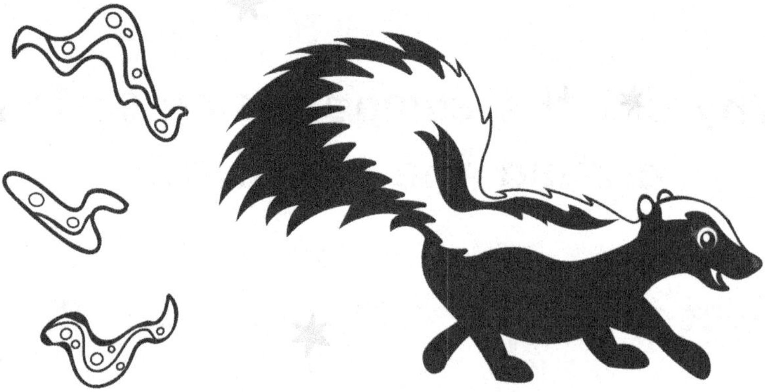

What do you call a boy who casts spells on other campers?

Harry!

What happened when the camp barber got lost in the woods?

The campers started combing the area!

What do you do about a tree that keeps moving around?

You planter!

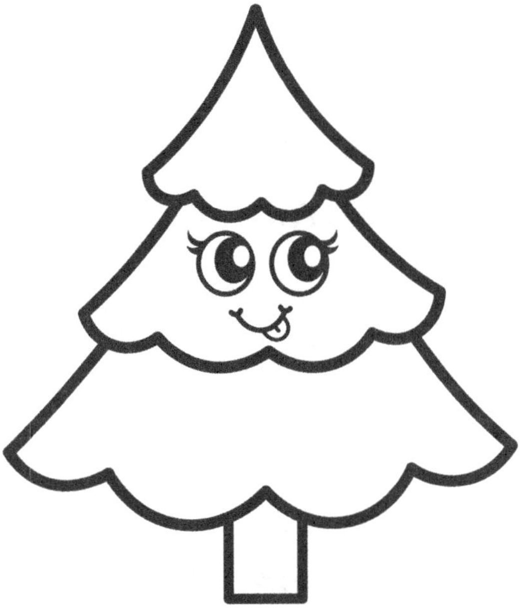

How do trees make so many friends?

They branch out!

Why was the water frustrated?

It was bottled up!

When do clouds have trouble with their memory?

When they are foggy!

What kind of shoes do spies wear on a hiking trip?

Sneakers!

What do you call a girl who goes to the beach a lot?

Sandy!

Why were the kids happy with gymnastics camp?

The counselors were bending over backwards for them!

What do you call a boy who only goes up to his knees in the river?

Wade!

What do you call a Russian moose?

A Moos-cow!

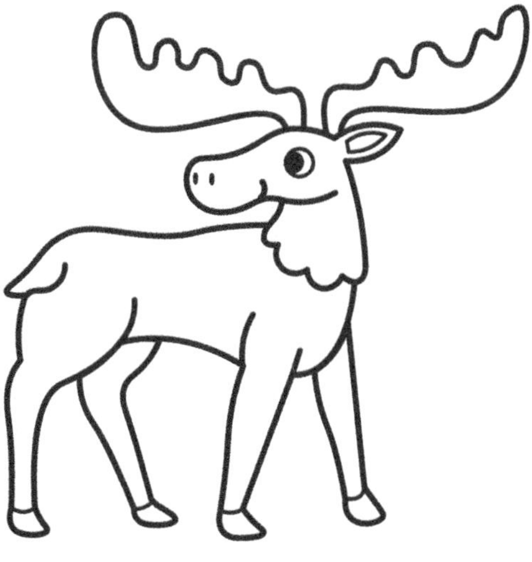

Why are fish afraid of computers?

They are afraid of getting caught in the internet!

Why do tents keep their money in the bank?

Because they are always being held up!

Why did the campers lose the tug of war contest?

They were at the end of their rope!

Why couldn't the tree solve the puzzle?

It was stumped!

Who is the first one out of the tent in the morning?

Up and Adam!

Why couldn't the camper see the eagle?

Because it was in da skies!

Why did the campers bring their cat to camp?

They needed a first aid kitty!

Dad

Look kids, a flock of deer!

Kids

Herd of deer, Dad!

Dad

Of course I've heard of deer,
there's a flock of them
over there!

Who helps Santa's elves at
Christmas time?

The Toy Scouts!

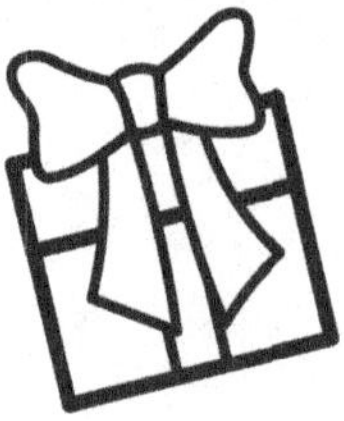
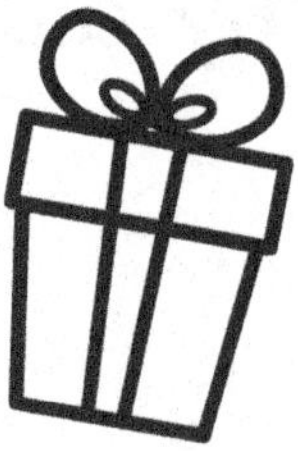
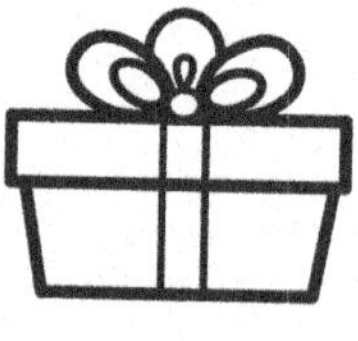

What do you call a girl who likes trees?

Willow!

Where does a snail go when it's raining?

A shell-ter!

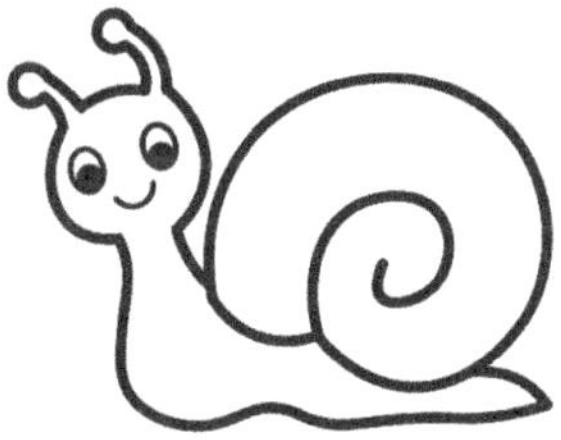

What do you call a snail on a sailboat?

A snailor!

What is the most important thing to pack for a camping trip?

Toilet paper!

What kind of birds should wear sunscreen?

Bald eagles!

How did scientists invent bug spray?

They started from scratch!

What do you call a girl who likes to win?

Victoria!

Why did the ant go to the camp doctor?

He was feeling low!

What do you call a turtle who takes lots of pictures?

A snapping turtle!

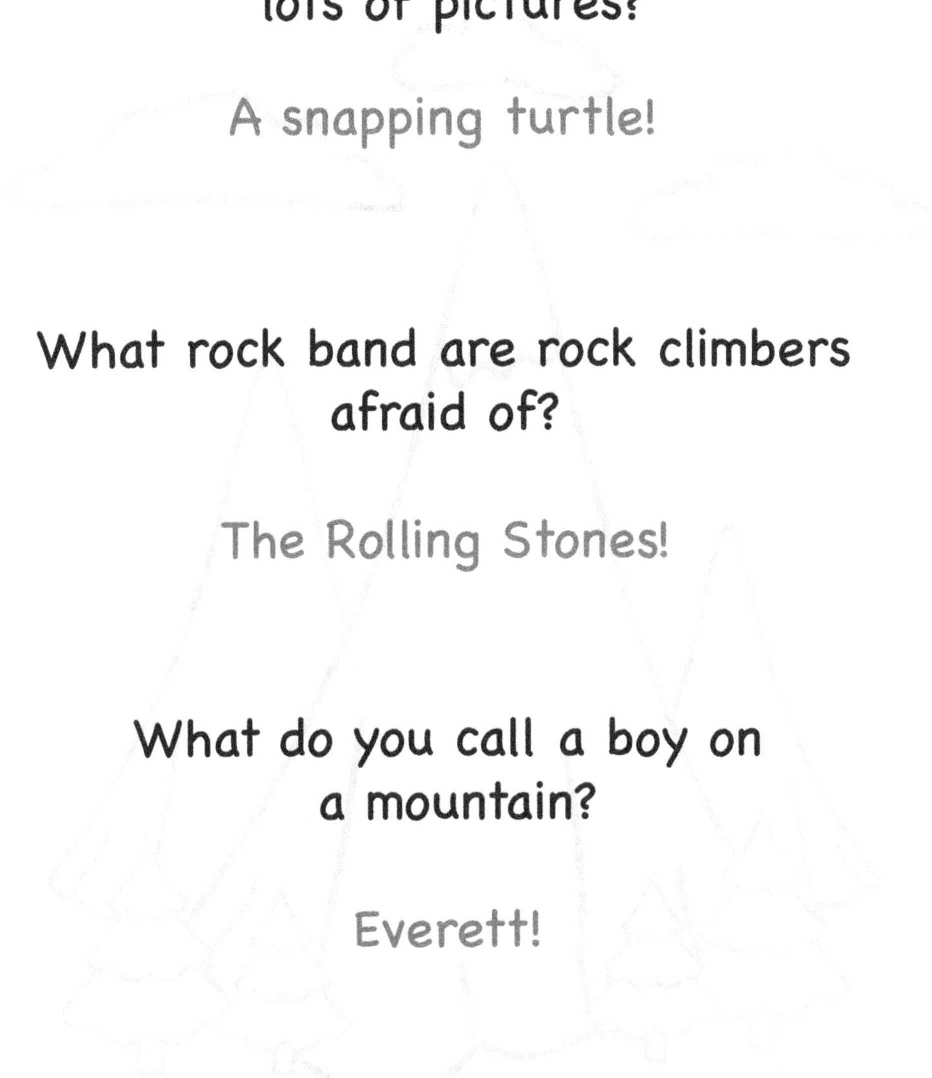

What rock band are rock climbers afraid of?

The Rolling Stones!

What do you call a boy on a mountain?

Everett!

How do trees sleep?

Like logs!

Camper 1

Remember the lunch that I couldn't keep down?

Camper 2

Let's not bring that up again!

What time is it when a ghost haunts your tent?

Time to get a new tent!

What do you call a boy who needs comfortable shoes?

Walker!

What song does
Smokey the Bear play
to help fight forest fires?

The Soaky Pokey!

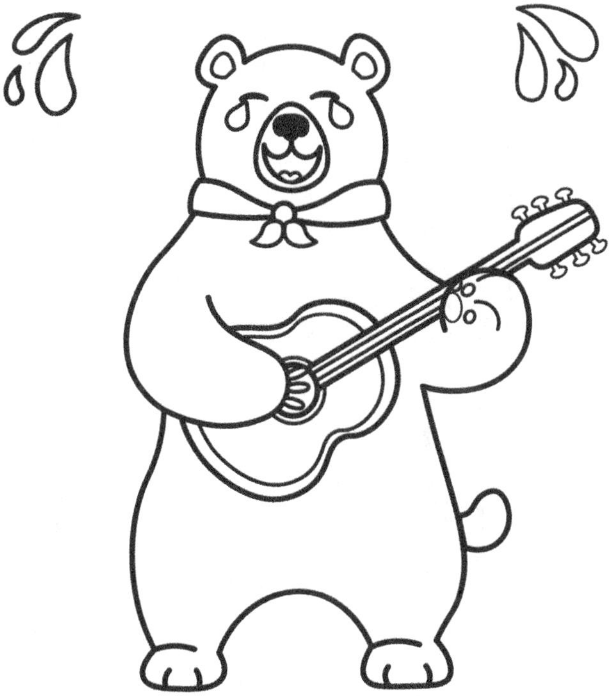

What do you call a boy who likes
hot dogs?

Oscar!

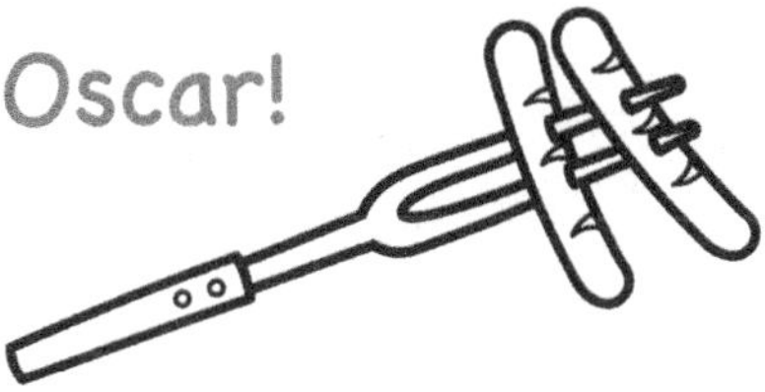

Why doesn't Bigfoot take selfies?

They always come in blurry!

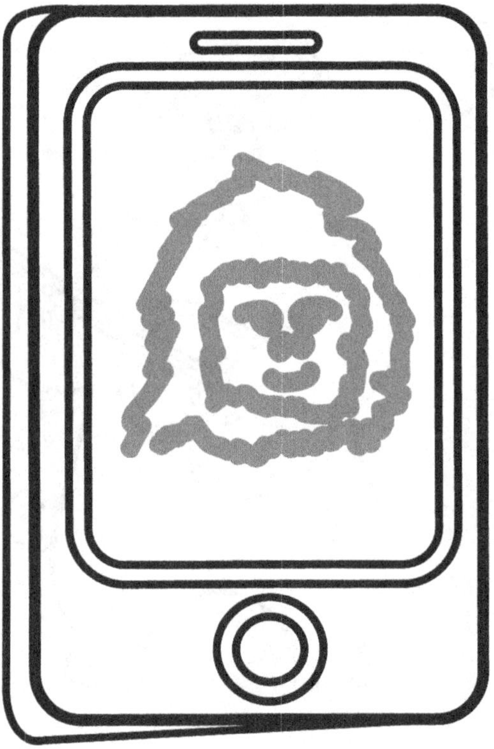

Why didn't the kids laugh at the vulture joke?

It was over their head!

There are ten campers in the tent,
all but nine went for a hike.
How many were left?

Nine!

What do you call a girl who
likes oysters?

Pearl!

What kind of dance do the campers
go to on July 4th?

An Indepen-dance!

What do you call a boy who likes
horseback riding?

Colt!

What do you call rabbits on a camping trip?

Hoppy campers!

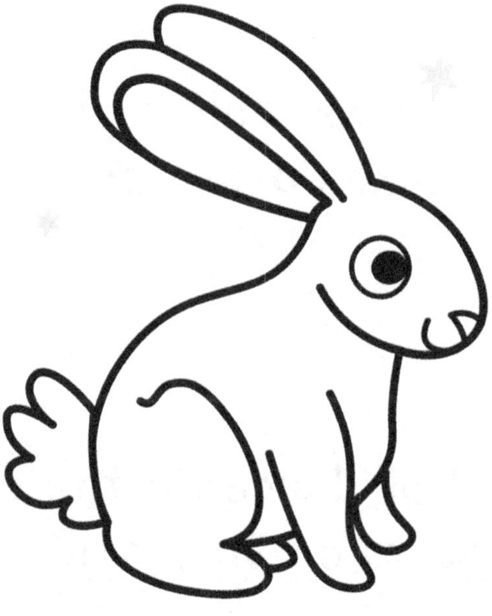

How did the campers learn how to make spaghetti?

They used their noodle!

What happened when the campfire got mad?

It blew its cool!

What do you need to do if you want to go to computer camp?

Get with the program!

What do math teachers sing at camp?

Kum-Pi-Ya!

What kind of shoes do mice wear when they go hiking?

Squeakers!

What is the hardest part of learning how to ride a mountain bike?

The boulders!

Why couldn't the mountain bikes stay awake?

Because they were two-tired!

What school does a squirrel go to before kindergarten?

Tree-school!

What do you call a boy who likes fishing?

Finn!

What do you call a girl who likes Halloween?

Autumn!

What does a ghost need for archery camp?

A BOO & arrow!

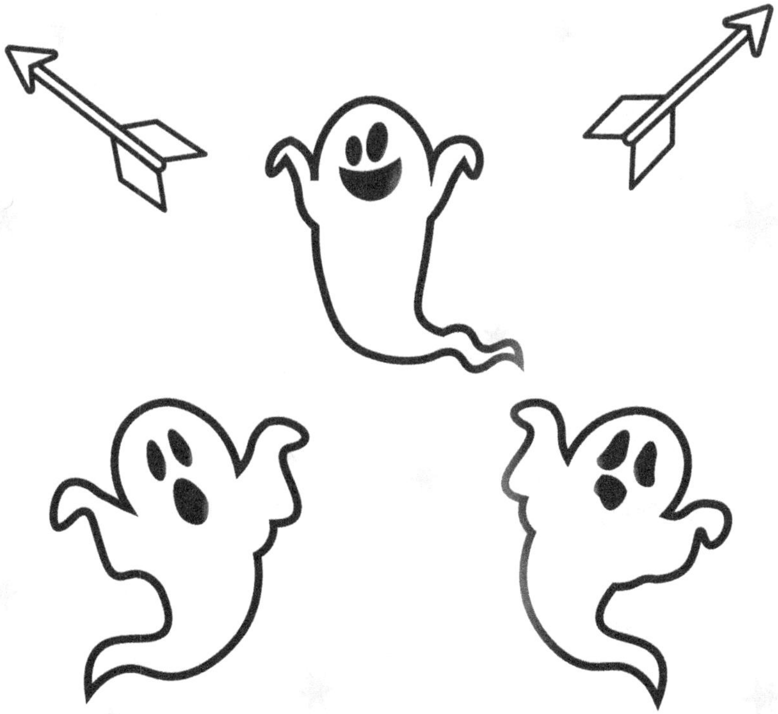

Where is Bigfoot going if he is wearing a bow tie?

A foot-ball!

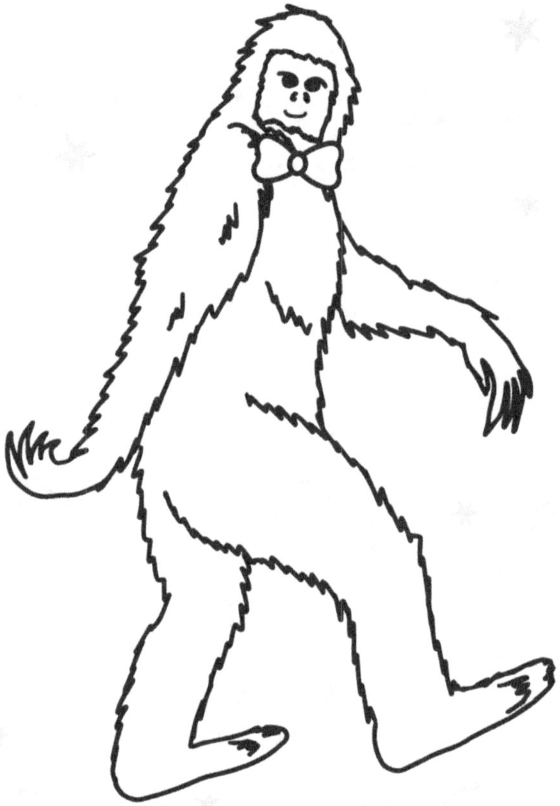

Why would Sasquatch make a good detective?

He can tell when something is afoot!

How do we know that the slugs ate all of the s'mores?

They were seen at the scene of the slime!

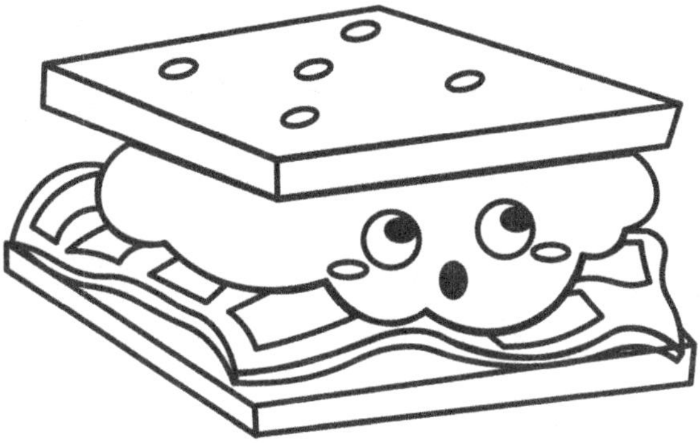

Why did the campers think the watermelon was crazy?

Because it was out of it's rind!

How do you treat a little mountain goat?

Like a kid!

Where do weather forecasters wish they could get married?

On Cloud 9!

Why didn't the rock climber trust the rope ladder?

Because they are always up to something!

What did the canoe team have for breakfast?

Boatmeal!

What do you call a boy who likes animals?

Noah!

What happens to little stars?

They glow up!

What is the best hiking spot
for apples?

Mt. Fuji!

What did the camp nurse say
to the bacon?

You're cured!

What is another name for
a sleeping bag?

A nap sack!

What kind of camp do creative pirates go to?

Arrrrrt camp!

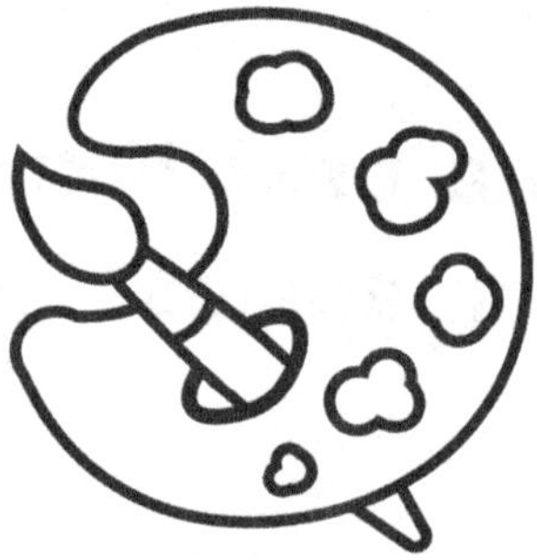

How does a bee like his eggs?

Honey side up!

What are the most famous insects?

The Beatles!

Why are unicorns a pain to go camping with?

They horse around too much!

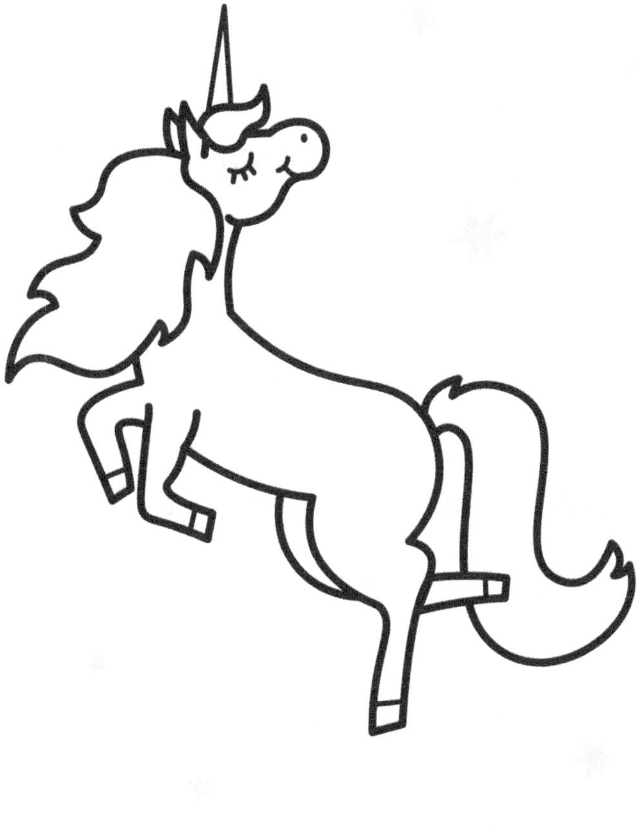

Why did the camper want to practice karate in the river's rapids?

Because the water was choppy!

Did you hear about the camper who went to buy a camouflage tent?

He couldn't find any!

Where do rock climbers like to go in New York City?

Rock-efeller Center!

Why don't campers like the top bunk?

They don't want to oversleep!

Why don't skeletons go rock climbing?

They don't have the guts!

What kind of books do you read in the outhouse?

Best Smellers!

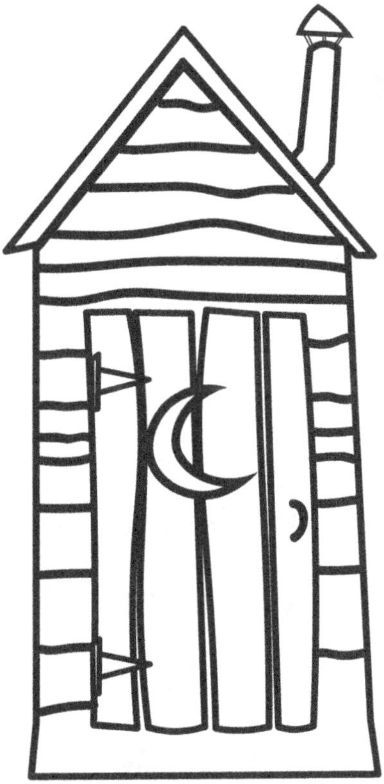

How many sides does an outhouse have?

Two, the inside & the outside!

Knock, knock.

Who's there?

Alpaca.

Alpaca who?

Alpaca the tents & camping stuff!

Knock, knock.

Who's there?

RV.

RV who?

RV there yet?

Knock, knock.

Who's there?

Yule.

Yule who?

Yule be sorry if you don't put on bug spray!

Knock, knock.

Who's there?

Scott.

Scott who?

There's Scott to be 100 mosquitoes out here!

Knock, knock.

Who's there?

Summer.

Summer who?

Summer excited about camp, summer not!

Knock, knock.

Who's there?

Canoe.

Canoe who?

Canoe believe how many mosquito bites I have!

Knock, knock.

Who's there?

S'more.

S'more who?

I want s'more s'mores!

Knock, knock.

Who's there?

Seymour.

Seymour who?

Do you Seymour mosquitoes outside?

What does a poop emoji cook over the campfire?

Poop-corn!

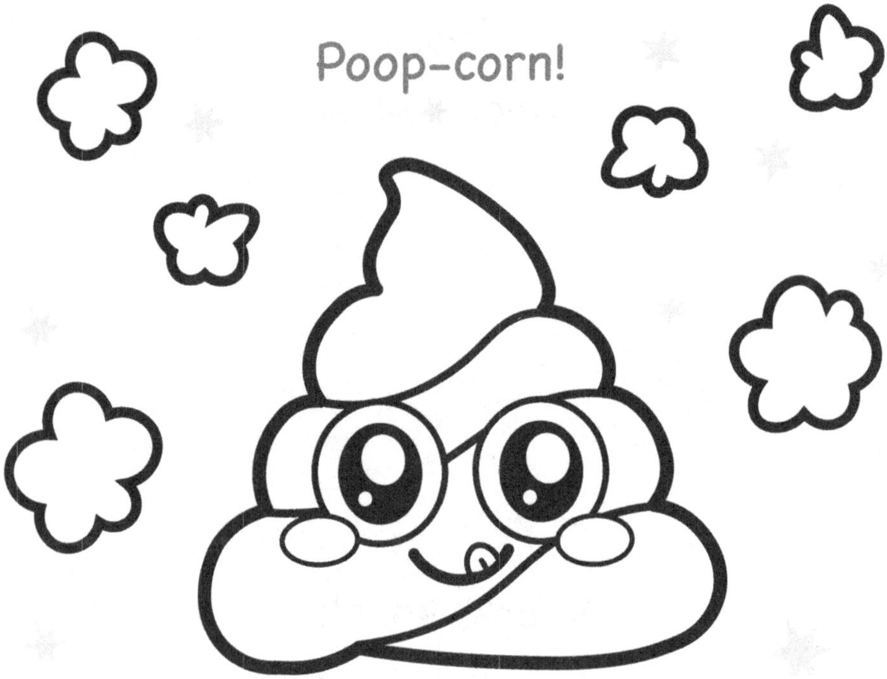

How is a walking stick made?

Whittle by whittle!

Did you hear about the peach joke?

It's pitiful!

Who kicked the raccoons out of the garbage cans?

The bears!

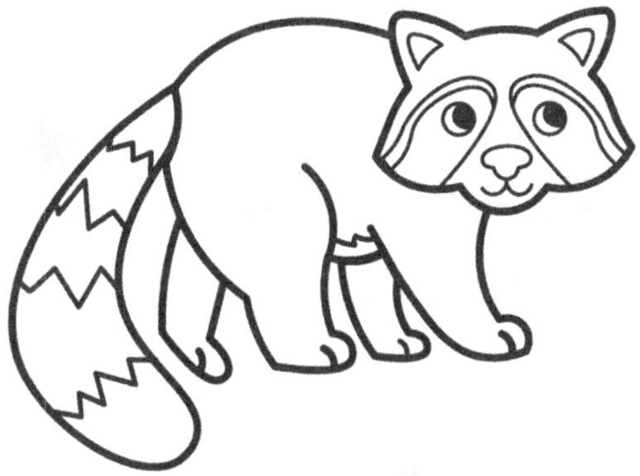

Camper 1

How did the pond get bigger this year?

Camper 2

Lake I know!

Who lives in a tree & eats french fries?

A frying squirrel!

Where do frogs keep all their books?

On their ipad!

Who doesn't like sitting around the campfire?

Yeti!

What kind of tent did dad bring on his camping trip?

A Pop tent!

Why was the snake lost?

He was rattled!

Why are mermaids afraid to go camping?

They don't want to get caught in a mosquito net!

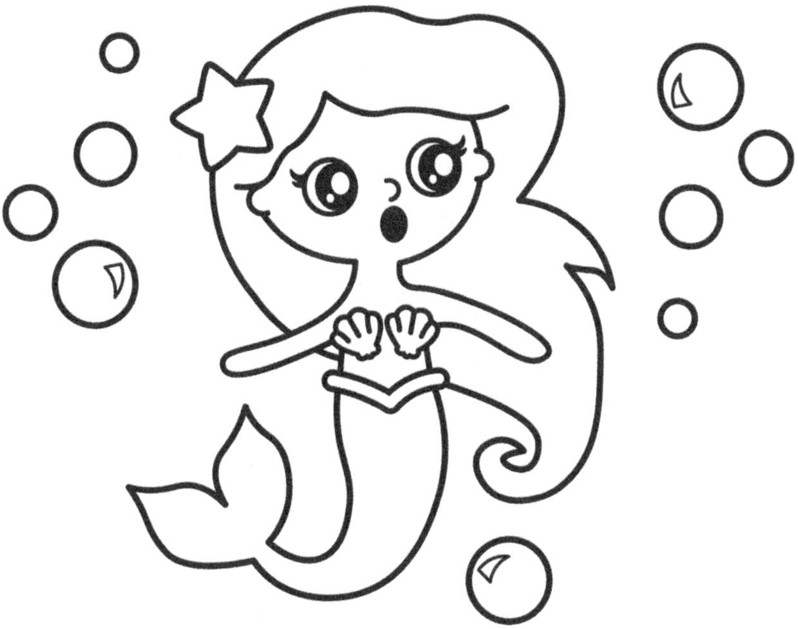

What kind of weather stinks when you are camping?

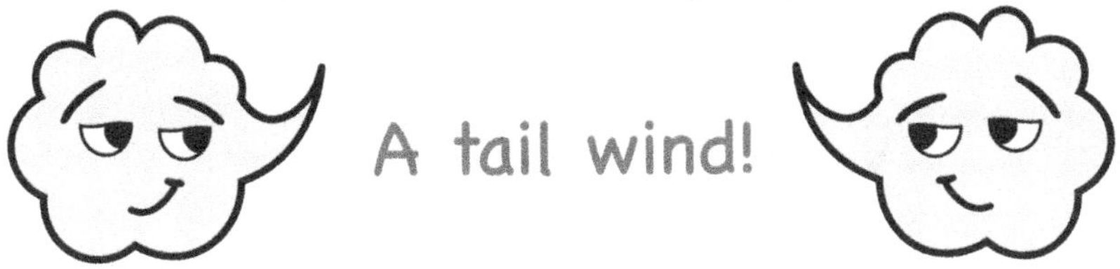

A tail wind!

What side of the tree does moss grow on?

The bark side!

What did the bumble bee counselor want from the campers after "lights out"?

Some bees & quiet!

What do ghosts like to do on a camping trip?

White water rafting!

What kind of music does soda like?

Pop music!

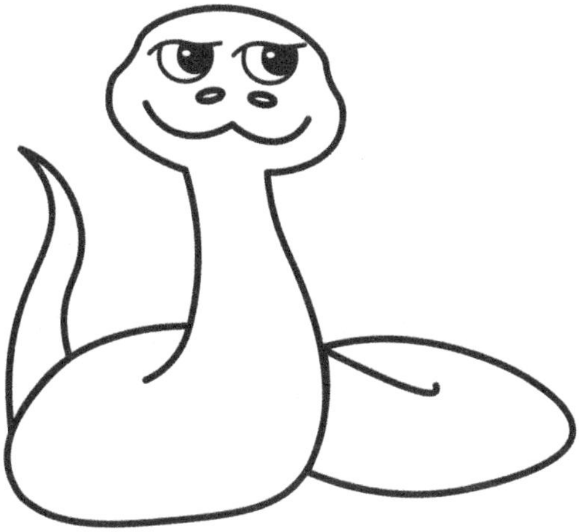

Why can't a snake win an argument?

It doesn't have a leg to stand on!

Why did the girl stay away from her brother's camp?

Boys 'n ivy!

Summer camp is a fun place to be...

If you are a mosquito!

What did the mosquito say to his friend?

Want to go out for a bite?

Why are campers interested in wildlife?

It is just their nature!

What does a bear say when he walks into his cave?

Honey, I'm home!

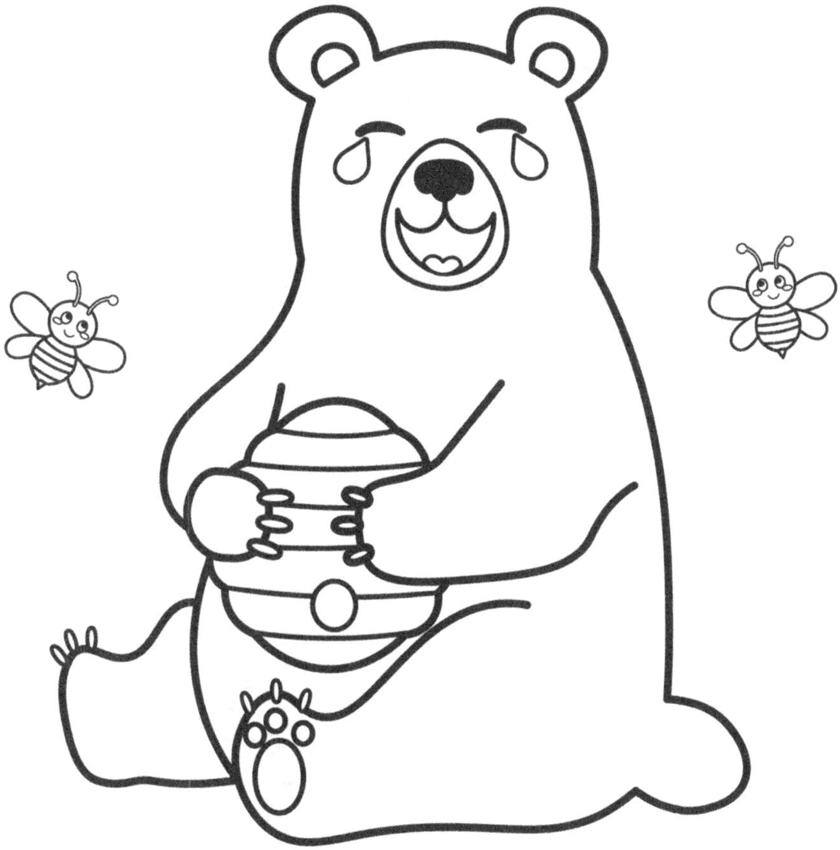

What do you call a mountain climber?

Cliff!

Where do the camp counselors get their archery supplies?

Target!

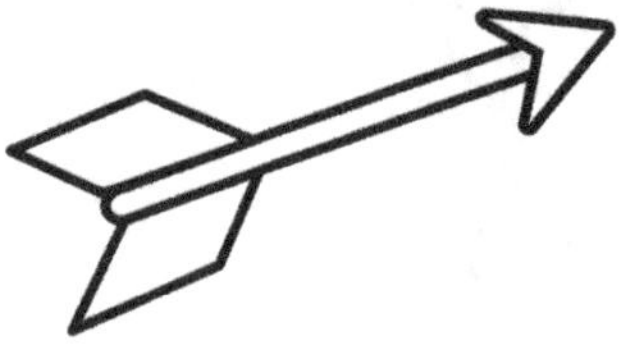

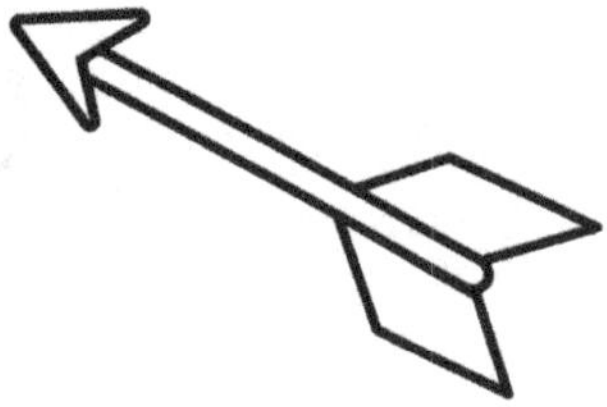

What kind of bicycle do poop emojis like to ride?

On a bicycle built for Poo!

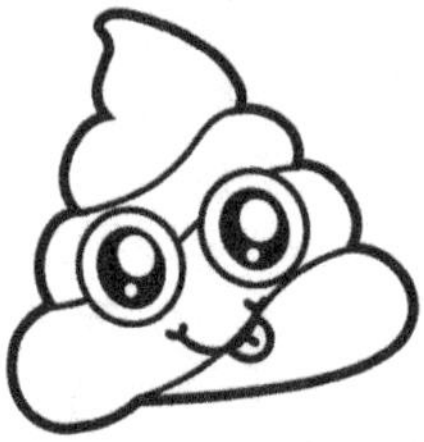

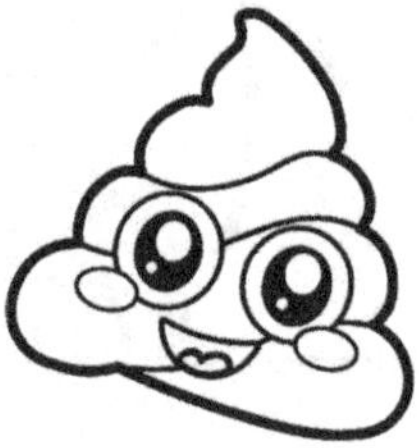

Why shouldn't you unplug a fan?

It will lose it's cool!

How bad were the mosquitoes at camp?

The SWAT team had to be called in!

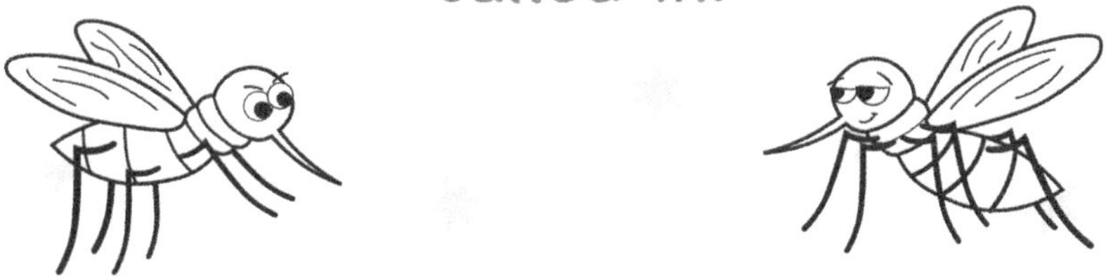

What do you call a depressed gnat?

A pestimist!

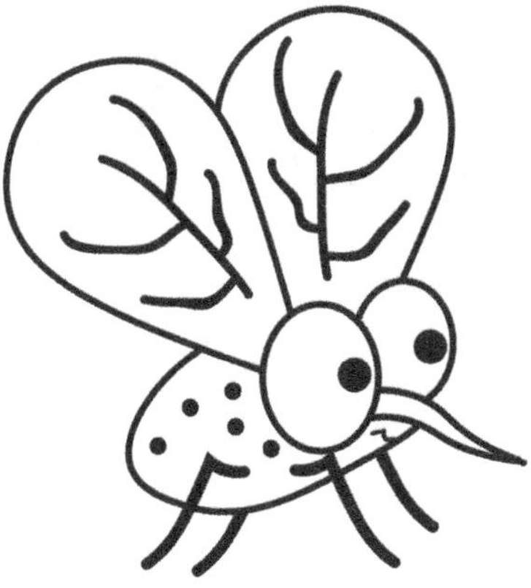

What kind of water is good for you?

Well water!

Why did the squirrel think he was nuts?

You are what you eat!

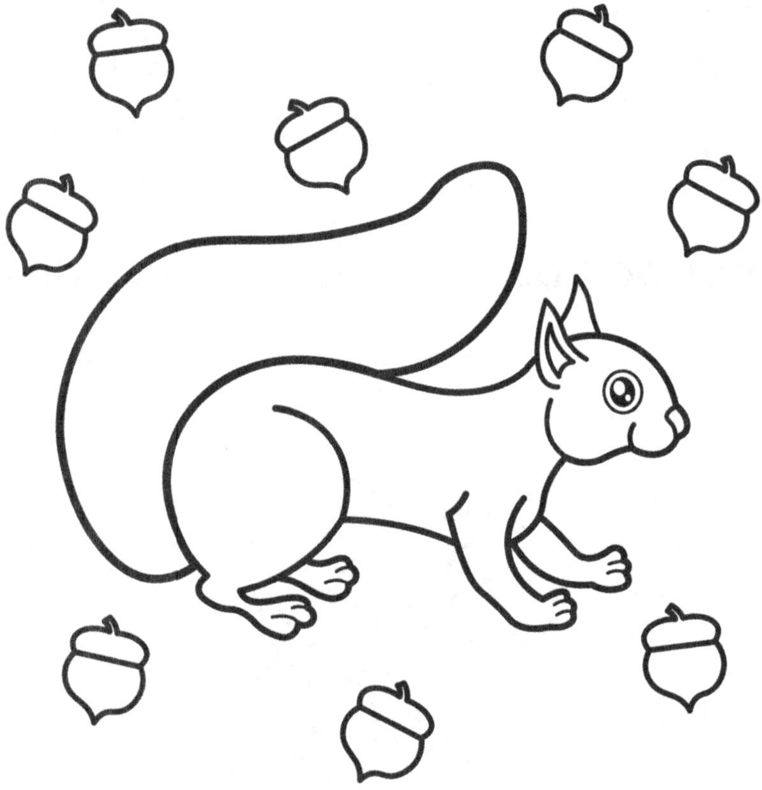

What is better than summer camp?

More summer camp!

What card game do you play
at camp?

Go Fish!

What is the biggest problem with
Girl Scout cookies?

No matter how many Girl Scout
cookies you eat, you always
want Samoas!

How do slugs send letters home
from sleep away camp?

Snail mail!

Why don't zombies have sleeping
bags in their tents?

They don't sleep!

RHYME TIME

What do you call a underground fart?

A root toot!

Where do bears practice yoga?

A Zen den!

What happens after you swallow soda?

A slurp burp!

What does a poop emoji sound like when he cries?

Poo-hoo!

Where is the best place to put a campfire?

A hot spot!

What do you call an unhappy little Girl Scout?

A frownie Brownie!

What do you call a melted marshmallow?

Ooey gooey!

What happens when it rains?

S'mores indoors!

What do you call a firefly
flying around at night?

A bright flight!

What do you call a campfire star?

A hot shot!

What does a bird do after dinner?

A chirp burp!

Who told the campers that
there is a swarm of mosquitos
coming their way?

An itch snitch!

What are the two reasons why campers don't like outhouses?

Number one & number two!

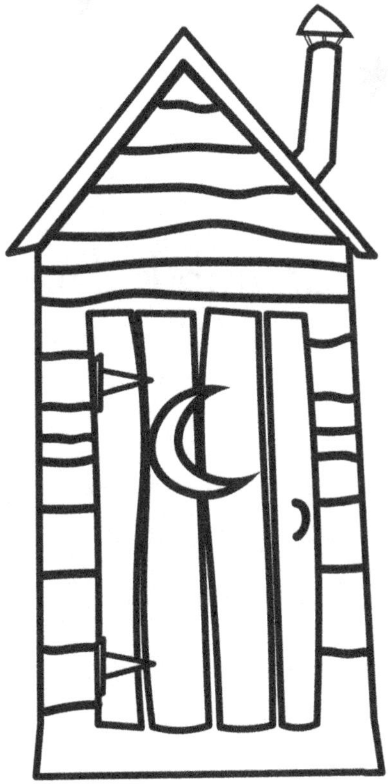

What side of the outhouse smells the most?

The inside!

What kind of bee is fun to bring on a camping trip?

A fris-bee!

Did you hear about the bed bugs who met in the mattress?

They got married in the spring!

Why was the silkworm a nervous wreck?

He was hanging by a thread!

Where do frogs keep their spare cash?

In the river bank!

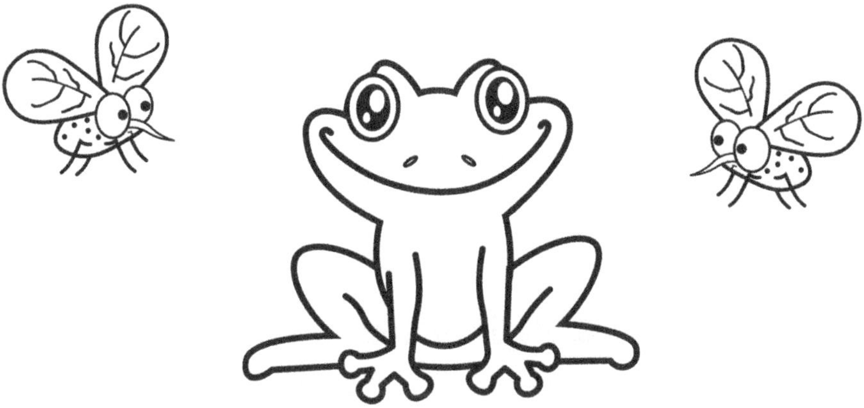

What flowers are frogs afraid of?

Tiger lilies!

What kind of soccer game do poop emoji's like to play?

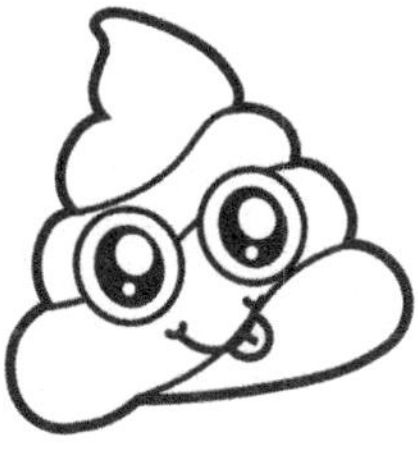

Poos-ball!
(Foosball)

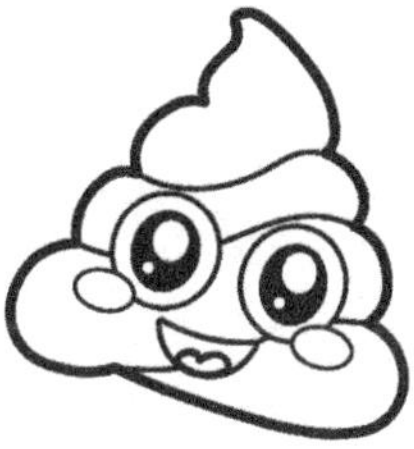

What is Smokey the Bear's favorite song?

The Smokey Pokey!

What happened when the campers used wet wood for their campfire?

It wooden light!

What do you call a camper that uses a walking stick?

Kane!

Son

Hey Dad, are you wearing my sunglasses?

Dad

No son, these are my dad glasses!

Where do celebrities go camping?

Holly-wood!

What does a warthog say to her rude children?

Tusk, tusk!

How do pine trees message each other?

Sapchat!

What kind of camp does Cinderella go to?

A sweep-away camp!

What do you say to rabbits on a hiking trip?

Hoppy trails!

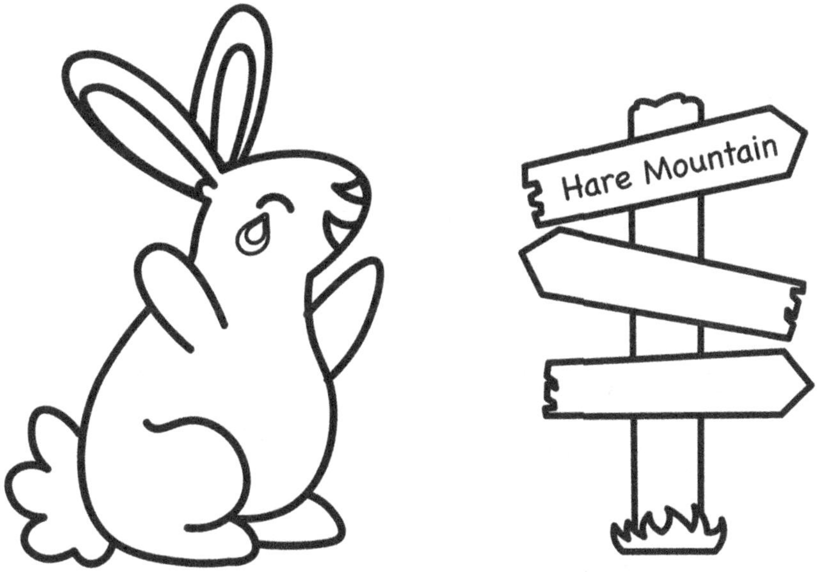

Why do baseball players make good campers?

They know how to pitch a tent!

Why don't bees fly to school?

They take the school buzz!

Why is a bee like a Sargent?

They both have stripes!

How do you play hide & seek at yoga camp?

Close your eyes & count to Zen!

Why are worms always looking for a deal?

Because they are dirt cheap!

What kind of potato chips do owls like?

Wise!

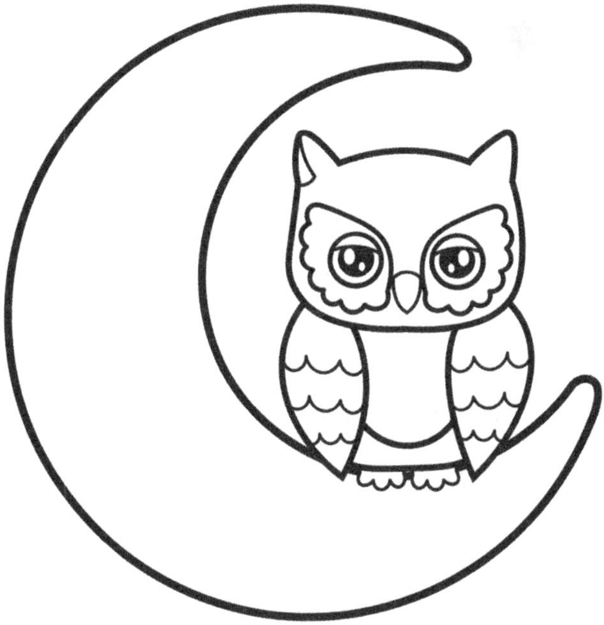

What did the fisherman sing when he was a little boy?

The reels on the bus go round & round!

What does a frog mechanic say?

Rivet rivet!

How do mosquitoes stay in touch
with family when they are
at sleep away camp?

Pestcards!

Why was the dog so good at
coloring between
the lines?

It was a border collie!

Where do superheroes buy
batteries for their flashlights?

At the supermarket!

What do ghosts drink on warm nights?

Ghoul-aid!

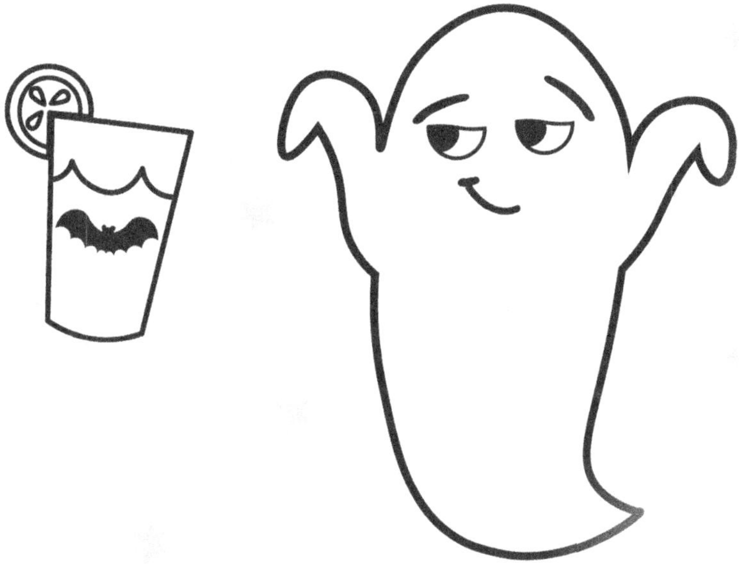

What do you send a witch at camp?

A scare package!

What did the spider want for lunch?

A burger & flies!

Why do shooting stars disappear so fast?

All good things must comet to an end!

Why did the boy pack dog food for his camping trip?

He was bringing a pup tent!

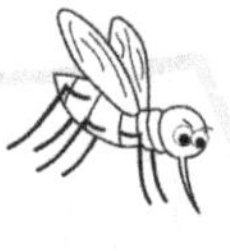

What is a mosquito's favorite sport?

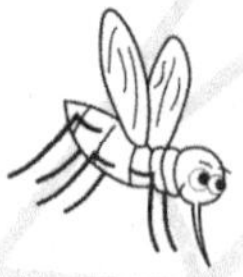

Skin-diving!

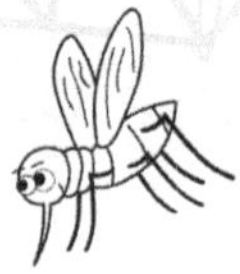

Why are campers so serious?

Because camping is in-tents!

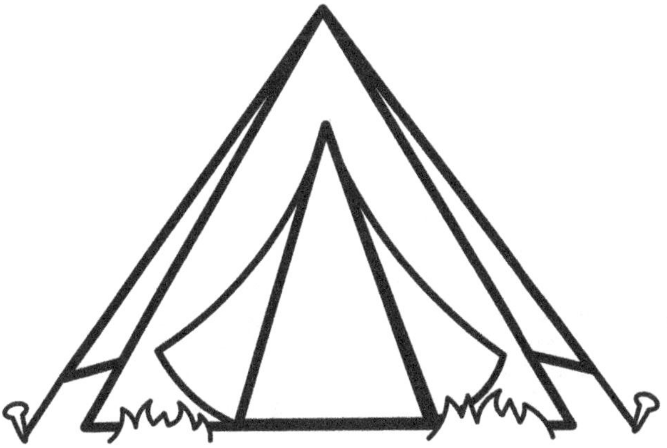

How did the pine trees fall in love?

It was love at forest sight!

What do you call a boy who likes
hiking across the USA?

Miles!

What do deers like to eat for breakfast?

Doe-nuts!

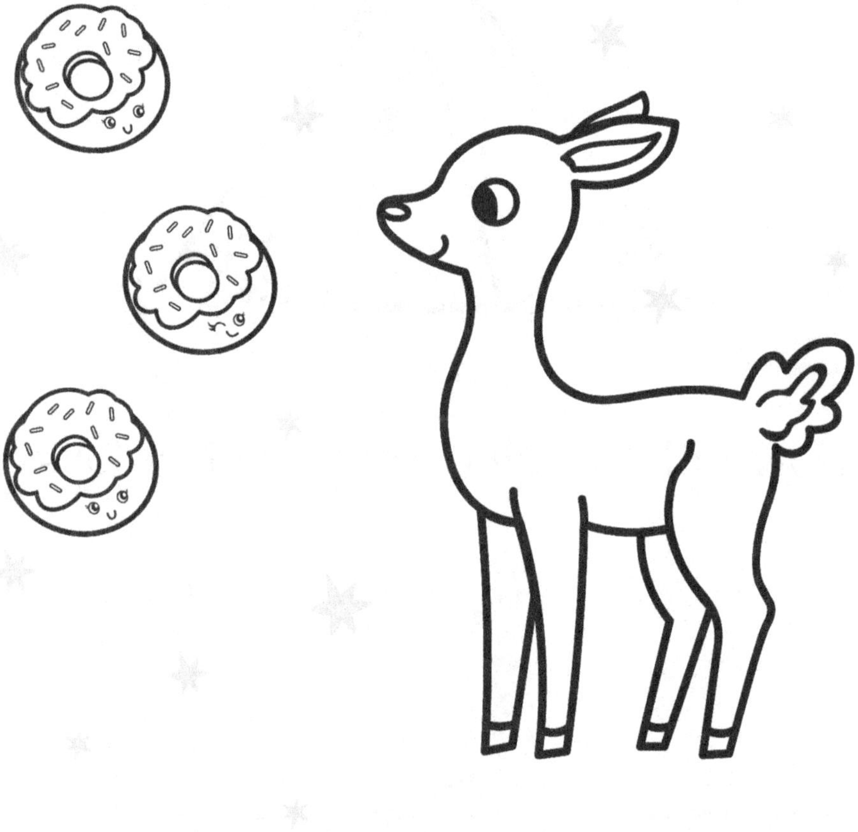

Why did the rope bridge come untied?

Knot sure!

How does a grizzly eat honey?

With his bear hands!

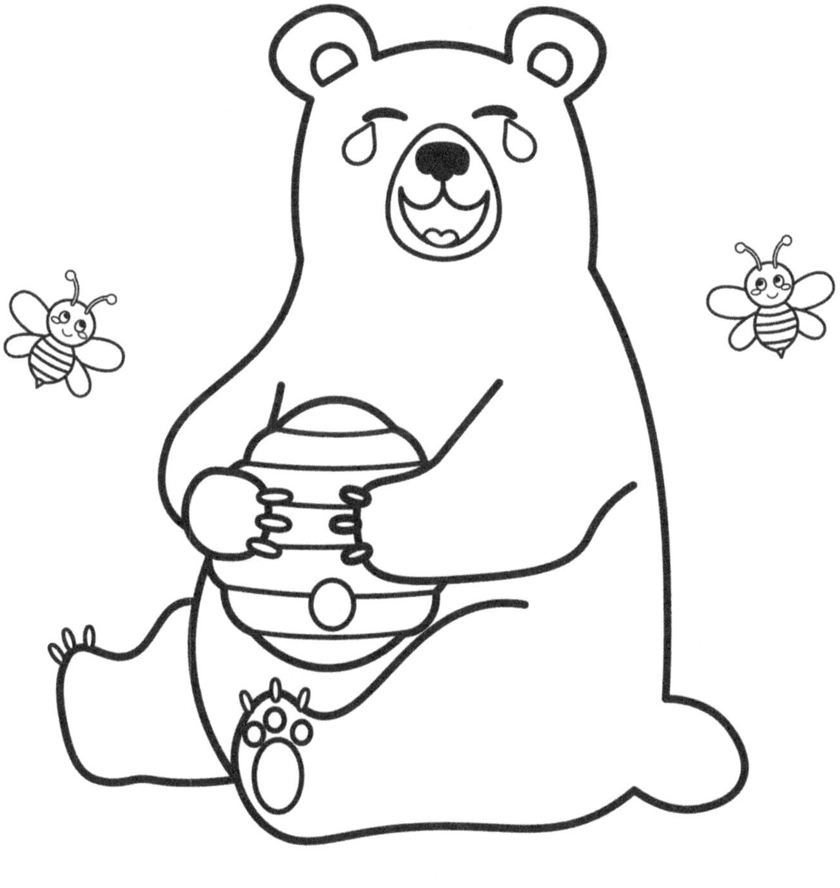

What song do chatty campers sing?

If You're Yappy and You Know it
Clap Your Hands!

What does a poop emoji pack for his camping trip?

Poo-jamas!

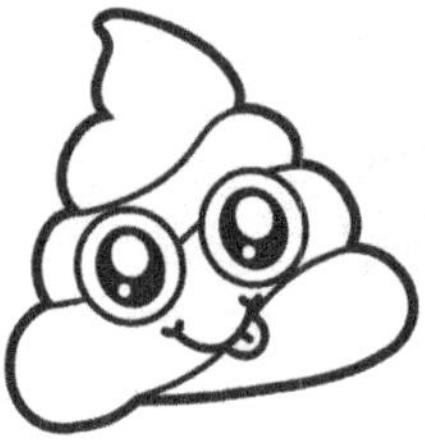

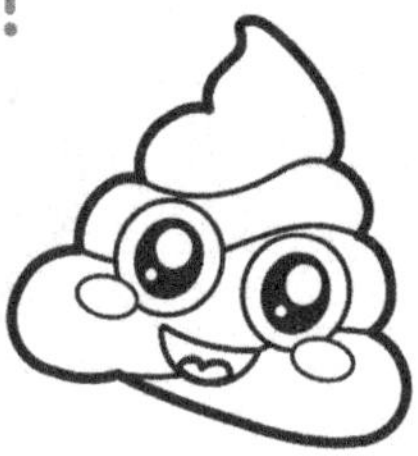

Where do bees keep their honey on camping trips?

In their honey belt!

What is a good song to sing at summer camp?

Bunky Town!
(Funky Town)

Why do forest trees make good cheerleaders?

They are always rooting for you!

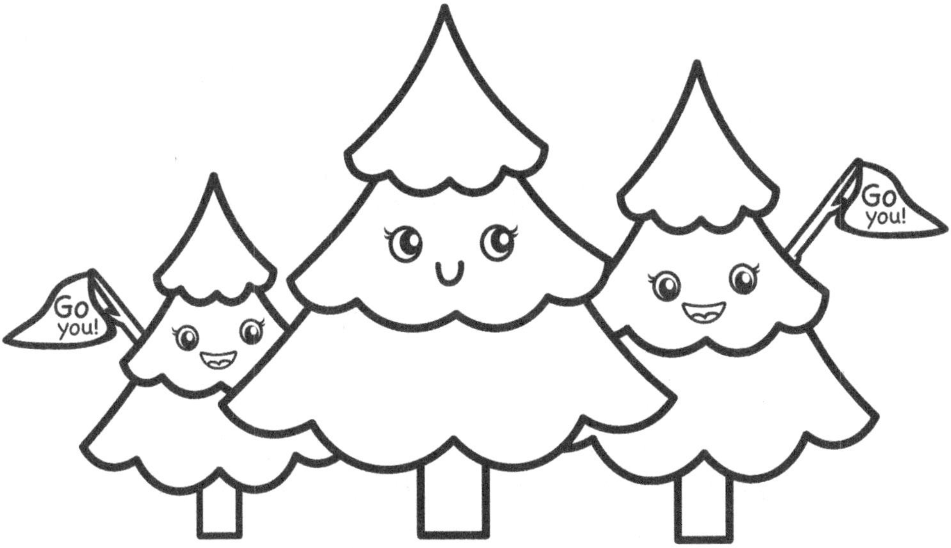

What does wet grass sing in the morning at camp?

Make dew friends, but keep the old!

Why did the camper bury his flashlight?

His batteries were dead!

What walks all day, smells, & sleeps with their tongue hanging out?

Hiking boots!

What do you call a nice girl climbing a fence?

Ivy!

What do you call a bad girl climbing a fence?

Poison ivy!

Why didn't the waffle go to the pancake party.

He was a square!

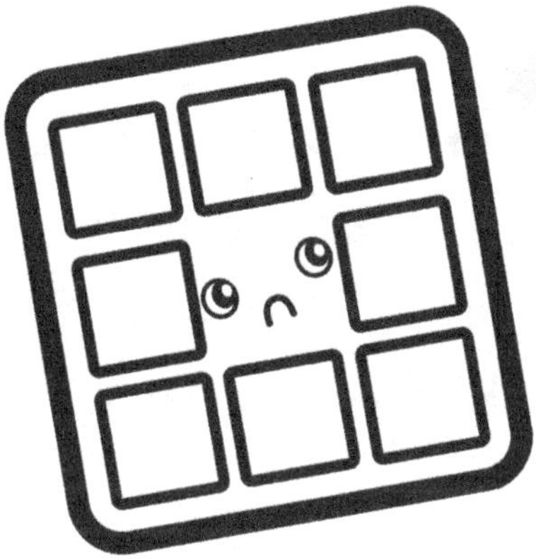

Why don't computer programmers like camping?

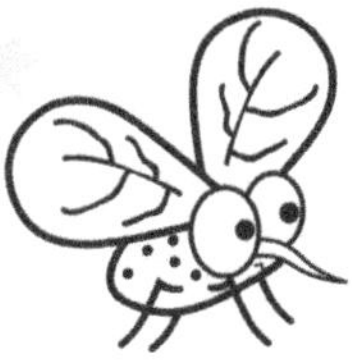

Too many bugs!

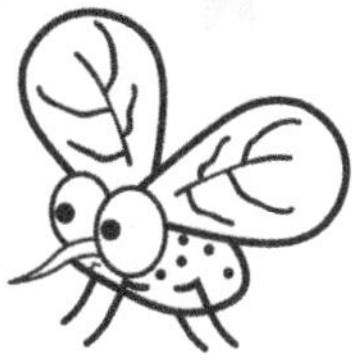

What do you call a girl who likes honey?

Bea!

Why don't bees sit down?

Their stinger is in the way!

Which is easier to spell, bees or bears?

Bees, it's spelled with more e's!

What did the tree say to the beaver?

Leaf me alone!

Why did the wild turkey cross the road?

Just beak-cause!

Why aren't llamas allowed to go to summer camp?

Too much llama drama!

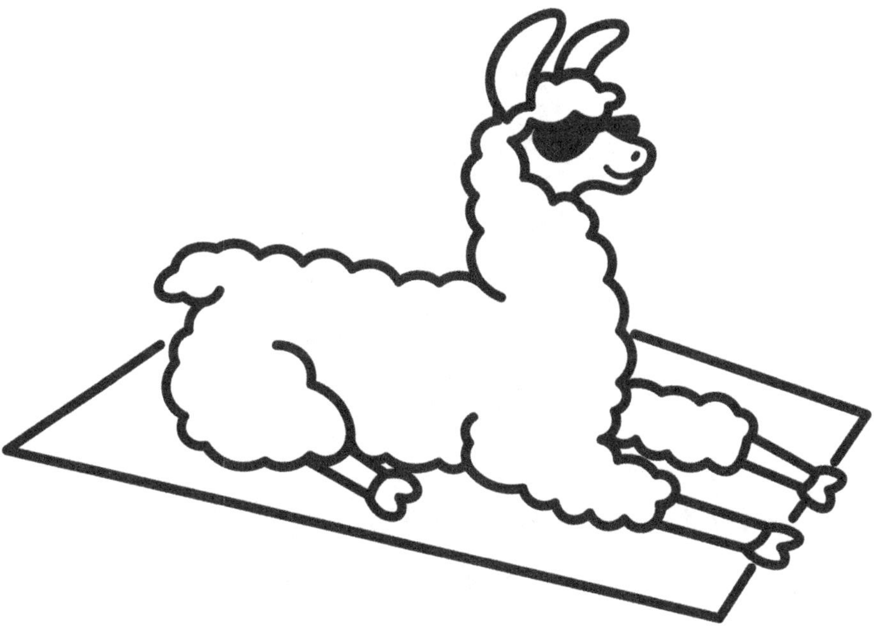

How did the pancake scare the campers?

It just crepe-d up on them!

Why wasn't the frog happy with his lunch?

There wasn't a fly in his soup!

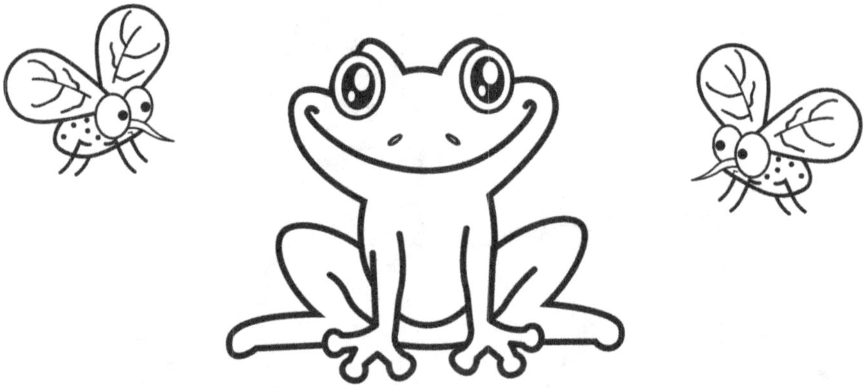

What do you call a girl who likes frogs?

Lily!

What did the quarterback say to the camper?

Hike!

What is the camp's motto?

The S'mores the Merrier!

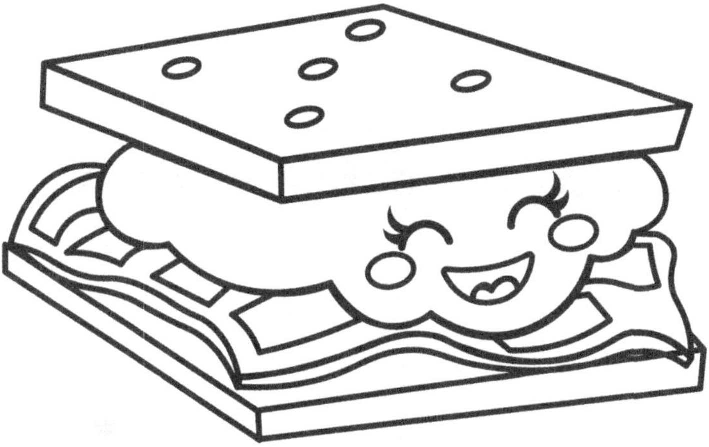

Camper 1

How do we find our way to the top of the mountain?

Camper 2

With our eyes!

What is the opposite of camping?

Glamping!

How do you define glamping?

Glamping is a fancy in-tents experience!

Is glamping like staying in a 5 Star Hotel?

No, it's like staying in a Billion Star Hotel!

What kind of coffee do you drink on your glamping trip?

A glamp-puccino!

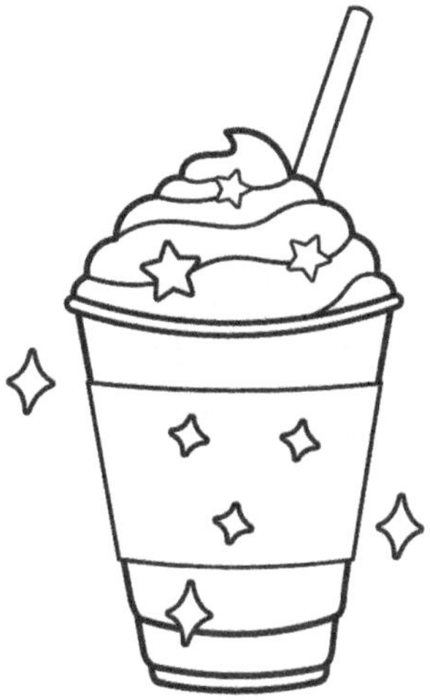

How do you relax on a glamping trip?

In a hot tub!

What is a glamper's favorite place to shop?

Park Avenue!

What do you call a cat that likes glamping?

A glamourpuss!

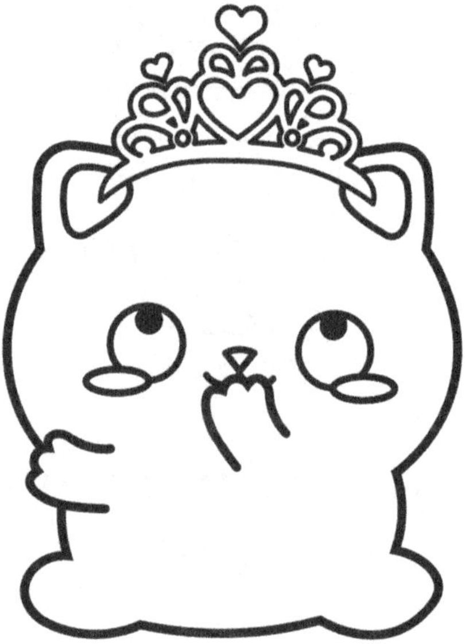

What kind of cheese do fish bring on their glamping trip?

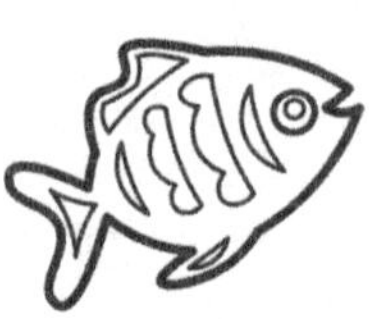

Mas-carp-one!

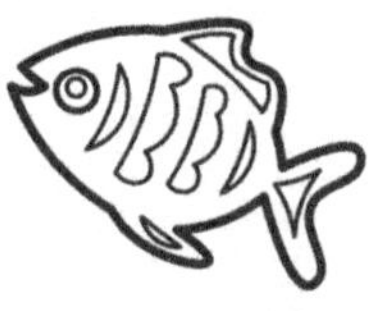

What do squirrels eat on a glamping trip?

Tree-course meals!

What kind of insects like to go glamping?

Ru-bees!
(Rubies)

Where do glampers roast their marshmallows

On a bonbon-fire!

How do you send photos of your glamping trip?

Insta-glam!

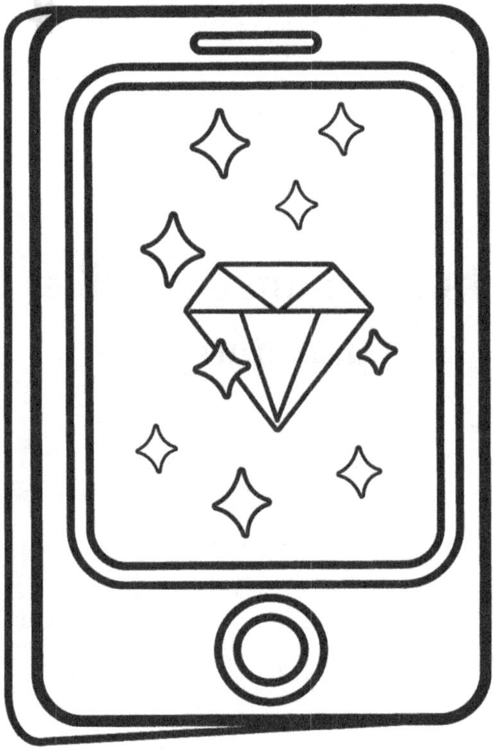

Why did the quarter go glamping without the penny?

Because it had more cents!

Why did the unicorn want to go glamping?

Because they have an all unicorn eat buffet!

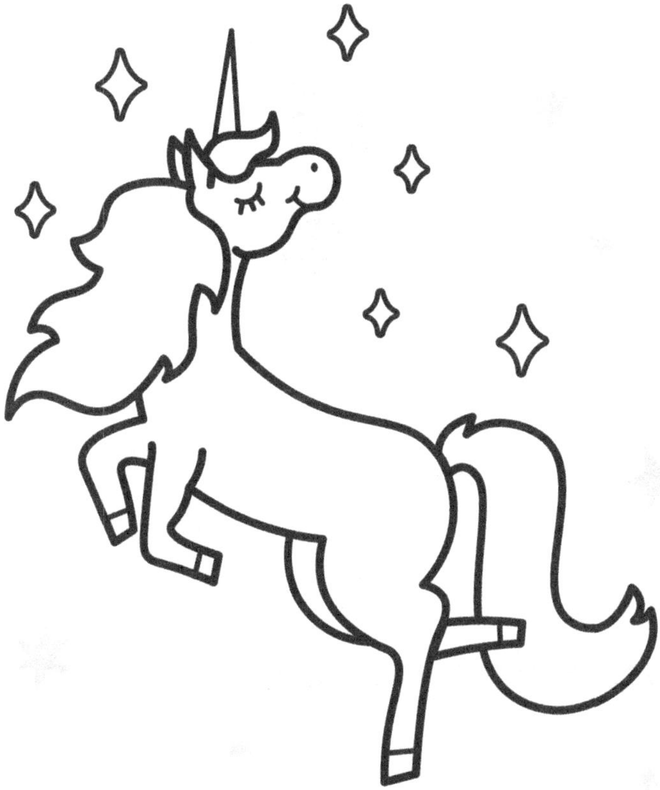

What kind of water do glampers drink?

Sparkling water!

What do ghosts bring on a glamping trip?

Mas-scare-a!

What do outer space glampers say?

May the quartz be with you!

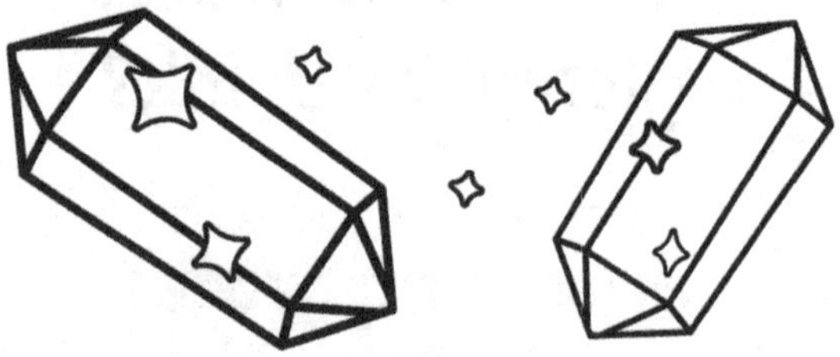

What kind of campfires do glampers have?

Saf-fires!
(Sapphires)

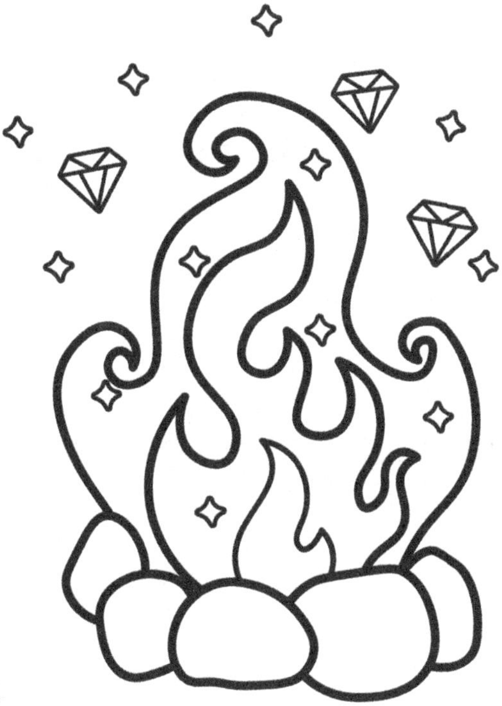

Where is a glamper's favorite place to relax?

Mount Ever-rest!

What group of young girls like glamping?

The Pearl Scouts!

What kind of sticks do glampers bring to the campsite?

Lipstick!

What is a camper's motto?

Camping Hair DON'T Care!

What is a glamper's motto?

Glamping Hair DO Care!

What do glampers call a lot of s'mores?

A s'more-gasbord!

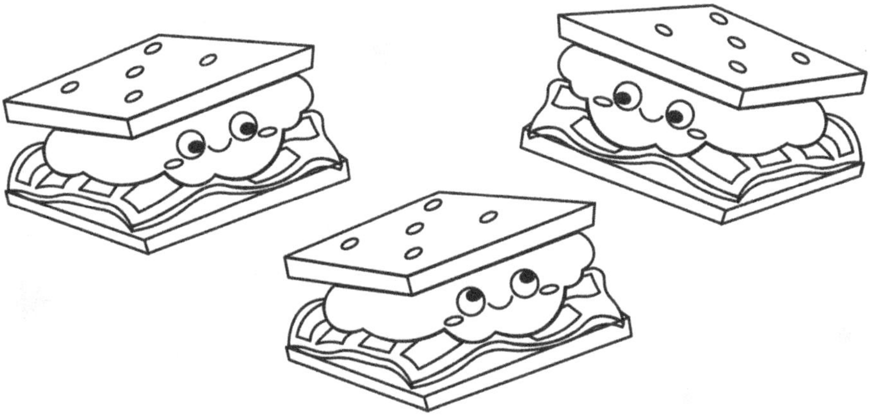

Where do rock climbers relax on glamping trips?

In rocking chairs!

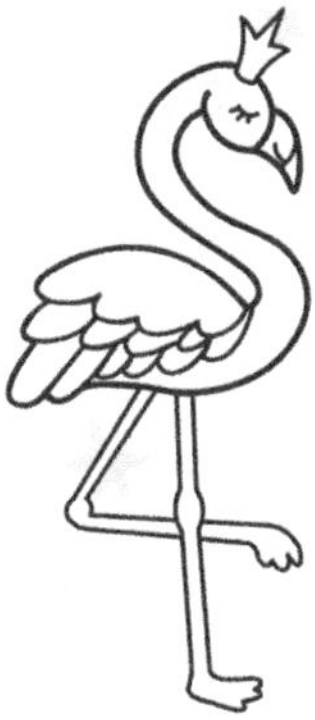

What kind of bird likes to go glamping?

A glamingo!

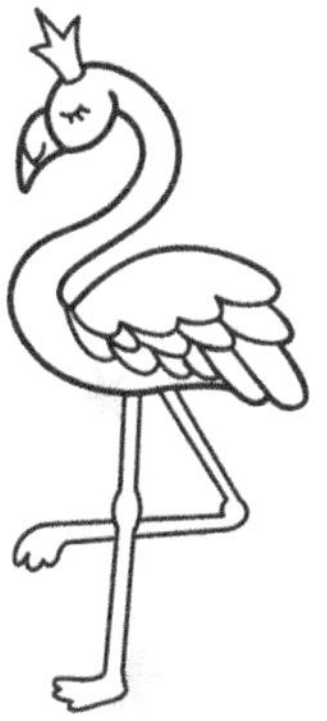

Why did the firefly go to the bathroom?

Because when you gotta glow, you gotta glow!

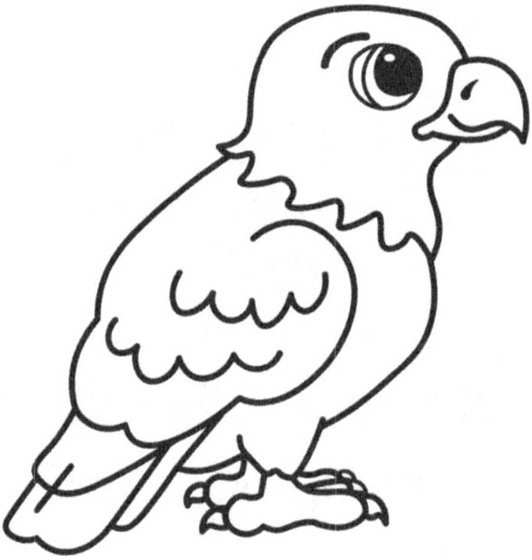

Why were the little eagles practicing their dance routine?

They were getting ready for the talon show!

What do you call an earwig on a zip line?

Ear-we-go!

What do you call a girl who likes springtime?

April!

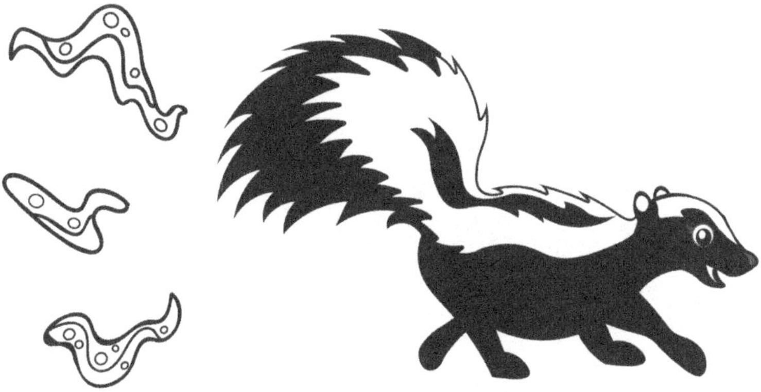

Why don't skunks need new cell phones?

Because they are never out of odor!

Did you hear about the family's camping trip last week?

It was in-tents!

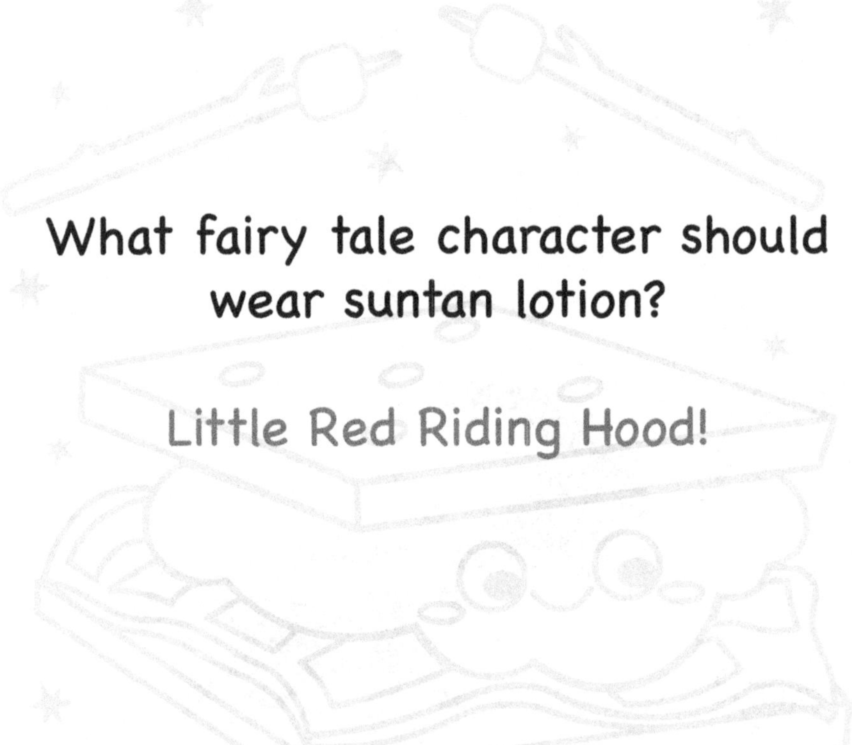

What fairy tale character should wear suntan lotion?

Little Red Riding Hood!

Have you heard about the s'more dilemma?

How can you ask for s'more when you haven't had one yet?

What do you call the cooking class at camp?

Home Ick!

Why couldn't the camper sleep?

He was having night-bears!

Why did the spider live in the computer?

Because he had his own web-site!

What bug sleeps the most?

A bed-bug!

How do bugs send photos?

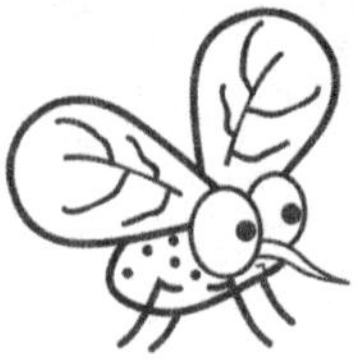

Snap-gnat!

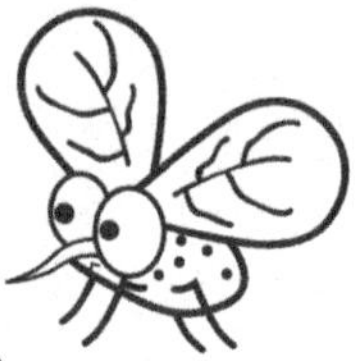

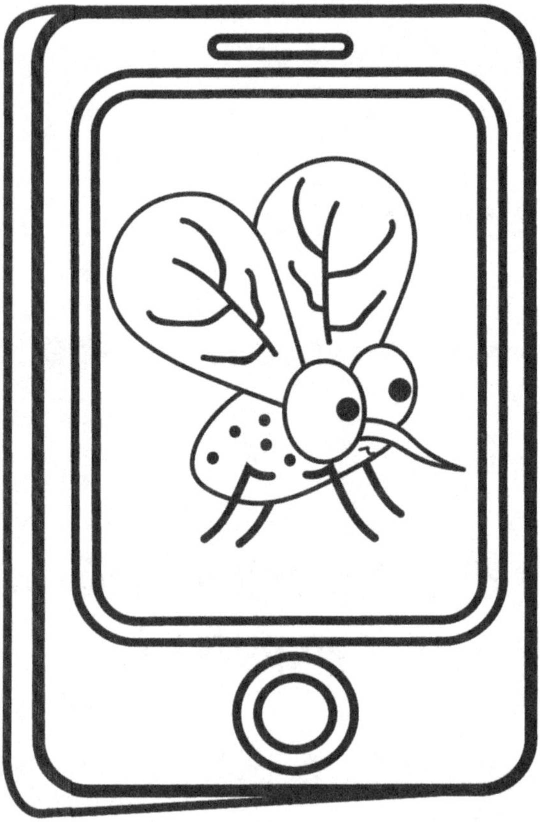

What always peels after a day in the sun?

Bananas!

What do campers do when it rains?

Play the Try Not to Laugh Challenge game!

How did the campers feel after hiking up the mountain?

Bushed!

How did the kids feel about football camp?

They were happy to tackle it!

What do you call a girl who likes running water?

Brooke!

What is a camper's greatest accomplishment?

Surviving the week without a cellphone!

How do you know if a camper is mad at you?

He'll tell you to take a hike!

What kind of camp does Sleeping Beauty go to?

A sleepaway camp!

Did you hear about the campground's canoe race?

It was a big oar deal!

What do little Boy Scouts drink out of?

Sippy cubs!

What did the squirrel say after she gathered up all the acorns?

That's all oaks!

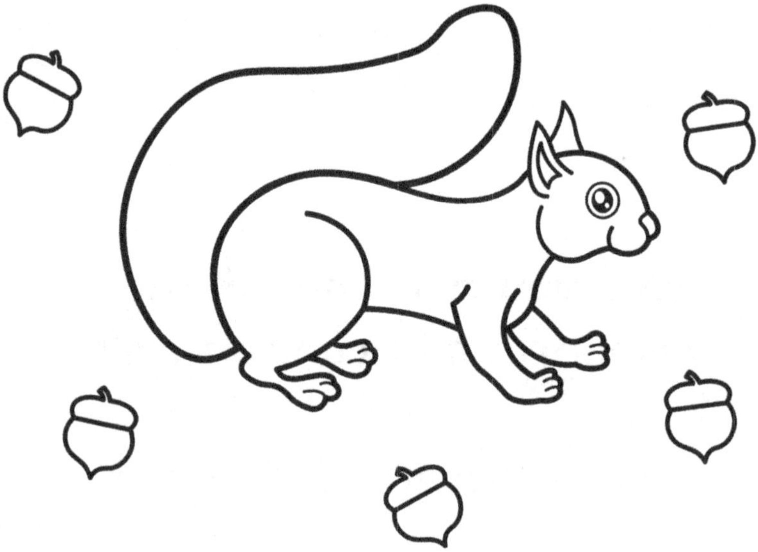

What are ladybugs afraid of?

Tiger moths!

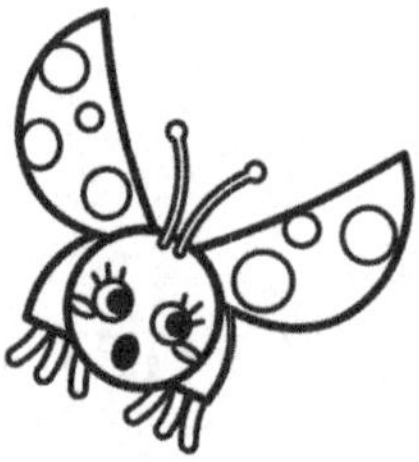

What has four legs & flies?

A horse on a hot day!

Why should you tell a moose a joke?

They are easily a-moosed!

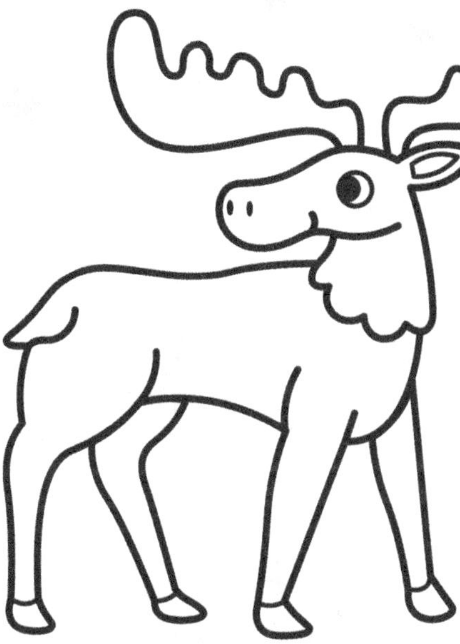

Who sells Girl Scout cookies at Halloween time?

The Ghoul Scouts!

Who eats the Ghoul Scout cookies?

The Cookie Monster!

What is a toad's favorite camp song?

The Croaky Pokey!

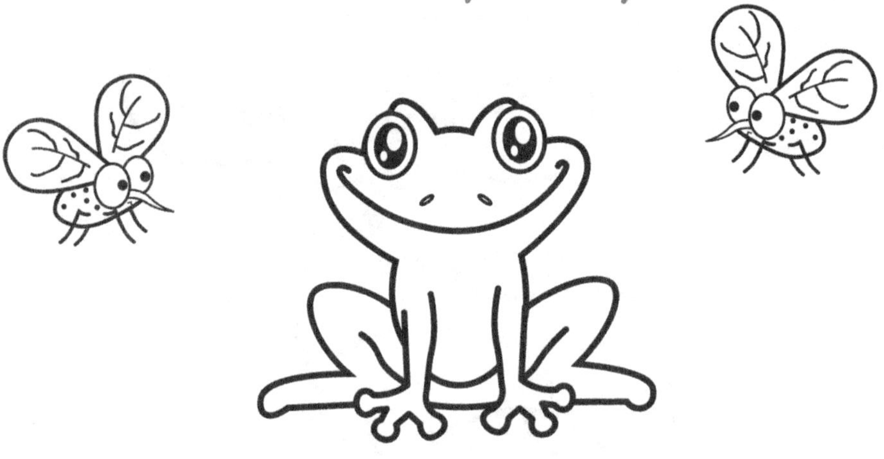

What did the rope bridge say to the campers?

Are you coming over?

What do you call a boy who is good at making s'mores?

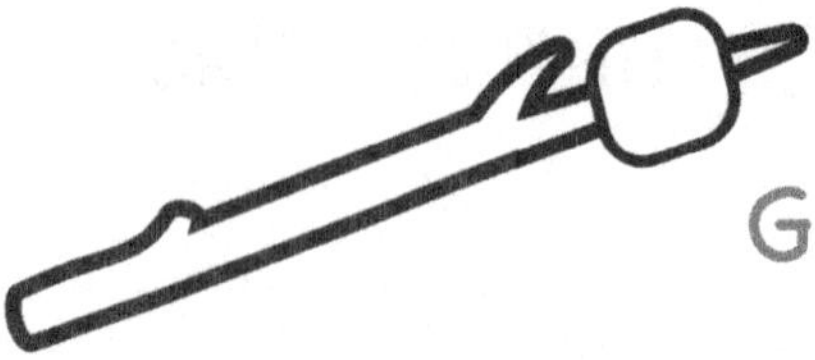

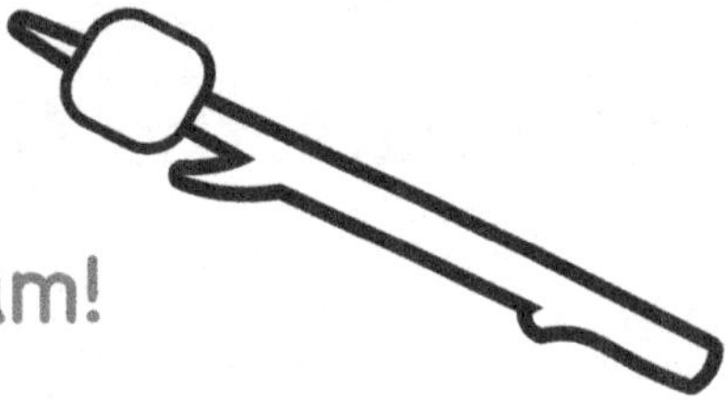

Graham!

What is the best way to find flowers that are lost in the woods?

A petal detector!

What do you send a kid at church camp?

A prayer package!

What do you call a huge pile of cats?

A meowtain!

Why did the anteater get heartburn?

He ate too many fire ants!

What did the anteater take for his heartburn?

He took some ant-acid!

Why was the canoe having trouble finding a place to dock?

There was a lot of pier pressure!

The campers were fighting about where to pitch their tents.

It was a tents situation!

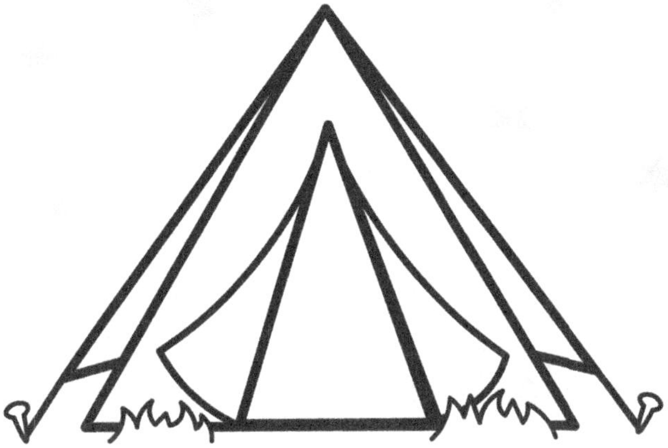

Why was the bungee jumper stressed out?

He was at the end of his rope!

Why do leeches need therapy?

Everything they get attached to tries to get rid of them!

Why did the kids want to come home from diet camp?

The program was wearing thin on them!

How do the Girl Scouts help the U.S. economy?

With Girl Scout Cookie sales!

Why did the Brownie go to the camp nurse?

She was feeling crumby!

How do you turn a boomerang into a stick?

Throw it down a one way street!

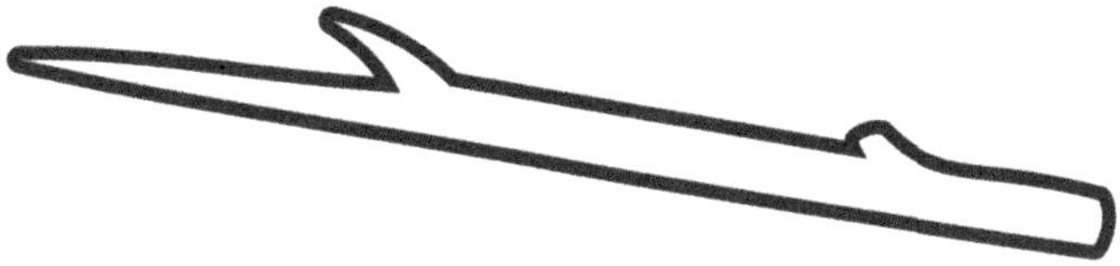

Why do farts stink at social media?

No one will follow them!

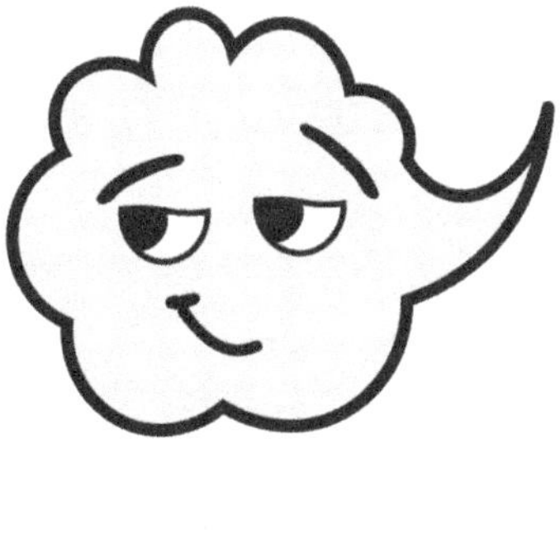

What do you call a boy who likes dinosaurs?

Rex!

Why were the kids happy with soccer camp?

They were having a ball!

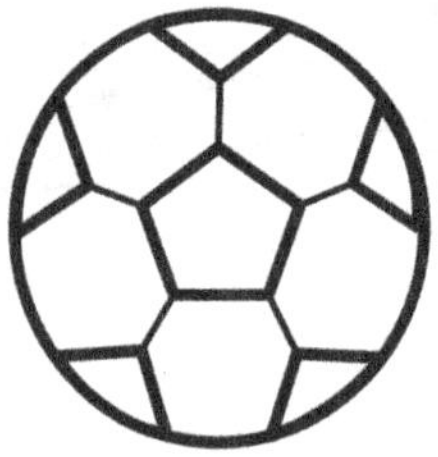

How do you make a pancake happy?

Butter him up!

What did the buffalo say to her little boy before he left for a camping trip?

Bi-son!

What was the last thing that went through the mosquito's head when he ran into the bug zapper?

His butt!

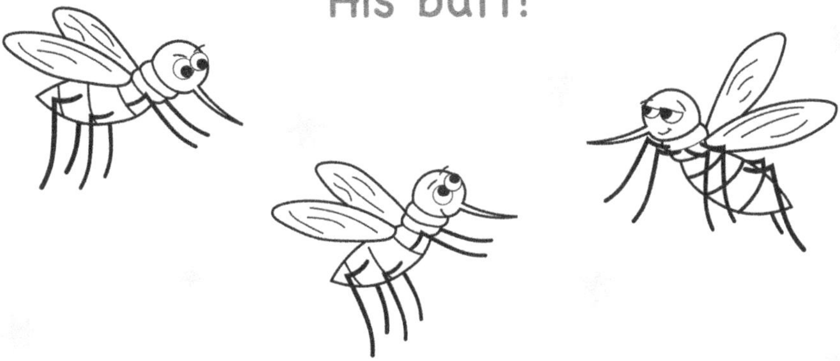

How do porcupines talk to each other?

Spine language!

How does a dinosaur feel after a long hike?

Saur!

What do you call a wolf lost in the woods?

A where-wolf!

Why are skunks so smart?

They have a lot of scents!

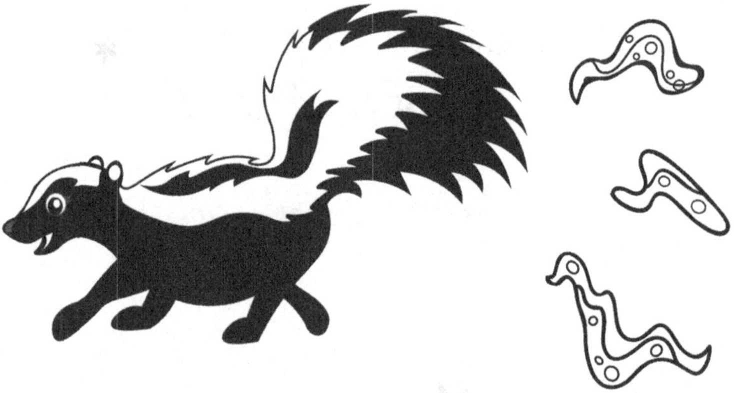

What do you call a boy who plays on the camp's baseball team?

Homer!

What park do you go to for relaxation?

A park bench!

Why didn't the mountain climber have to take any more climbing classes?

He had reached his peak!

What do snap peas listen to?

Pod-casts!

What do you call a grouchy lawn?

Crab grass!

Why couldn't the post office deliver the frog's mail?

He didn't have a zip toad!

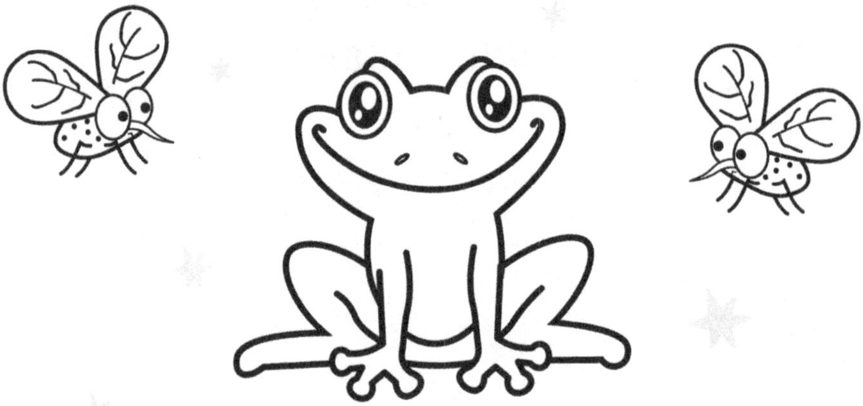

Why did the tree go to the dentist?

For a root canal!

What is a tree's favorite drink?

Root beer!

Why are fireflies always happy?

They look on the bright side!

What did the map say to
the other map?

Atlas, we found each other!

How does Bigfoot tell time?

With a sas-qwatch!

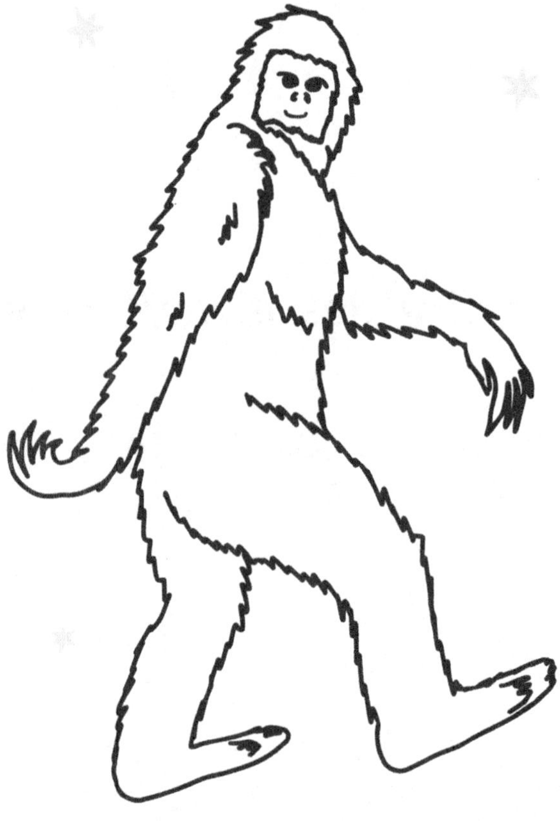

Why did the camper cross the road twice?

To catch a boomerang!

What did the kids think about baseball camp?

It was a grand slam!

We heard that the food at camp is great!

As long as you don't eat it!

What do you call a girl who likes watching the sunrise?

Dawn!

What does the camp baseball team & pancakes have in common?

They both need good batters!

Why do squirrels climb trees?

Because they don't have ladders!

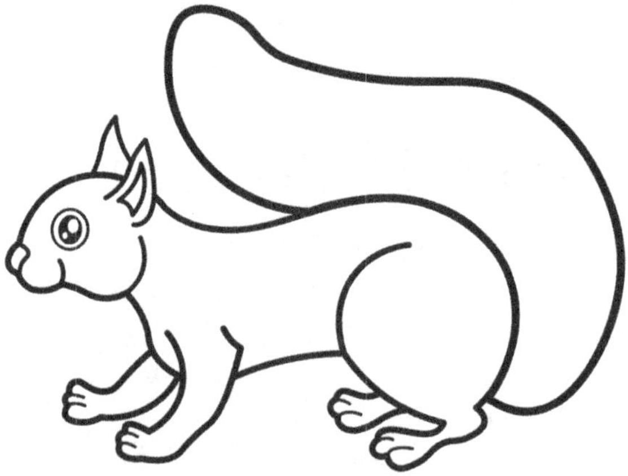

What do you put on your hot dog during a rainstorm?

Shower-kraut!

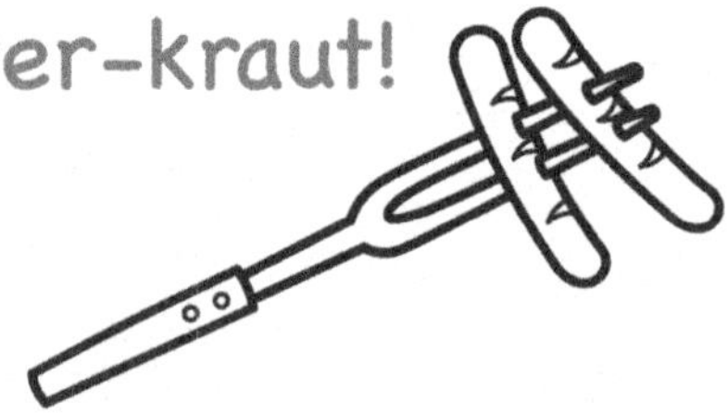

Why was the inchworm mad?

He had to switch over to the metric system!

What do moose like on their hot dogs?

Moose-tard!

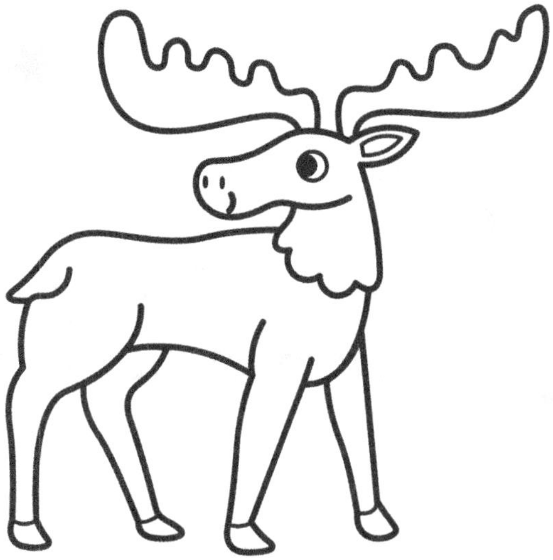

What game do moose play at camp?

Duck, duck, moose!

What kind of bow can't you use in archery camp?

A rainbow!

Why did the rock band go to art camp?

So they could draw a big crowd!

If you are good at fishing, would you be good at boxing?

No, because you only know how to throw hooks!

How do you know it is time to clean your tent?

When you need a compass to find your sleeping bag!

What is a camper's favorite drink?

A camp-puccino!

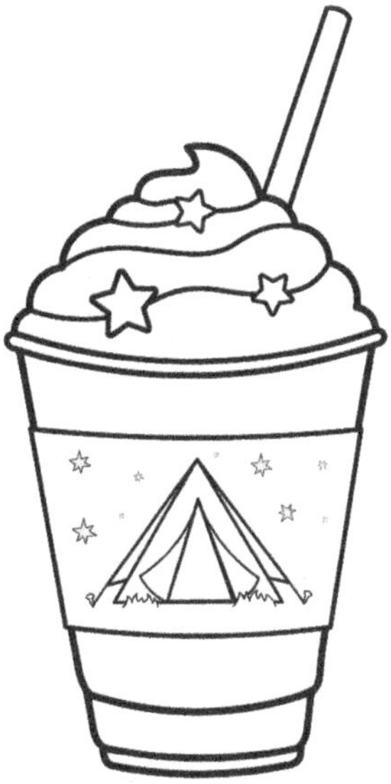

What do you call a boy who likes corned beef?

Reuben!

Why do chickens go on hikes?

To get some eggs-ercise!

The camper wasn't sure he remembered how to throw a boomerang.

And then it came back to him!

What do you call a girl who likes warm weather?

Summer!

What do you call a boy who likes lightning storms?

Benjamin!

Dad

Kids, be careful standing next to the trees in this campground!

Kids

Why?

Dad

They look shady to me!

What do you call a boy who likes to make camping videos?

Oscar!

What is the miracle of ice fishing?

You can walk on water!

Son

Dad, can you stop the car at the outhouse? I have to go to the bathroom!

Dad

Oh no, sounds like urine trouble!

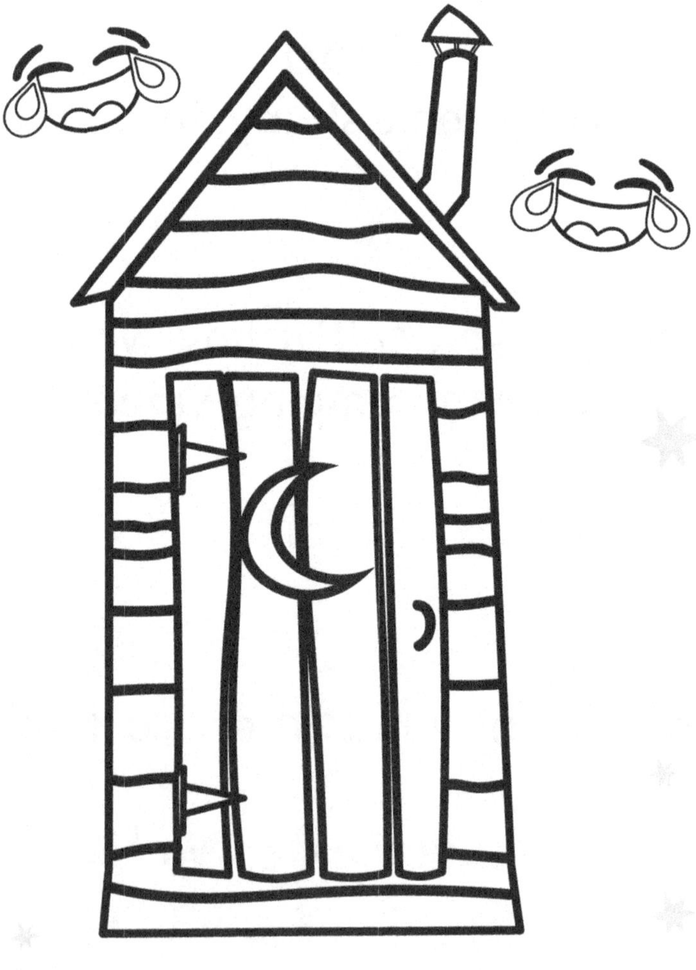

What do poop emojis eat on a hot day?

Poopsicles!

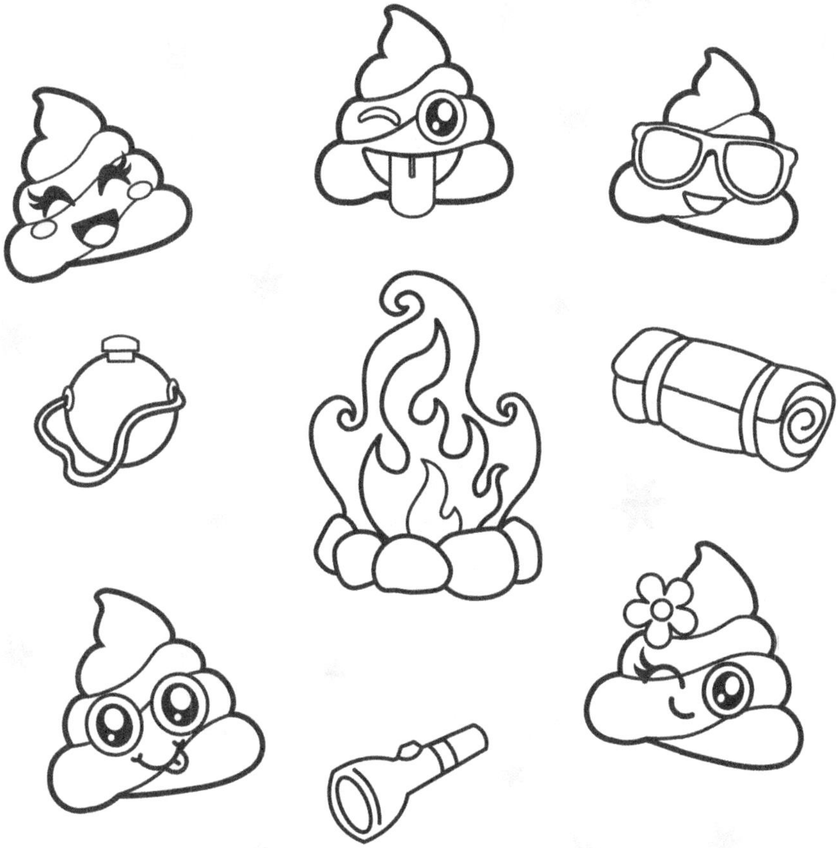

Why were the trees still at the campfire?

They wooden go home!

Why did the camper go to the doctor after a day of fishing?

He lost his herring!

What does a hot dog camp in?

In a wiener- bago!

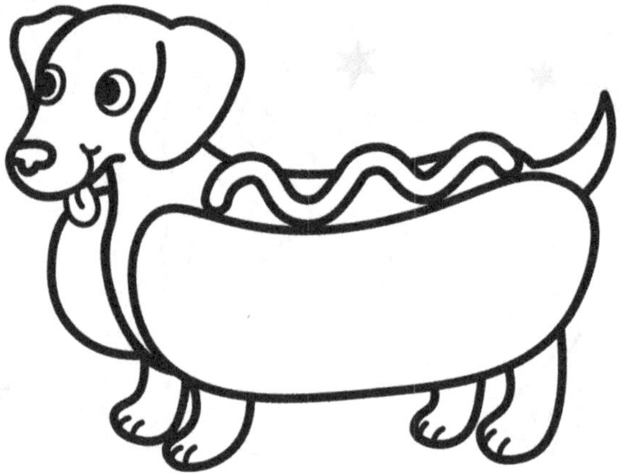

How much did the little trees like camp?

It was just oakay!

What did the llama say when something at the camp ate her dinner?

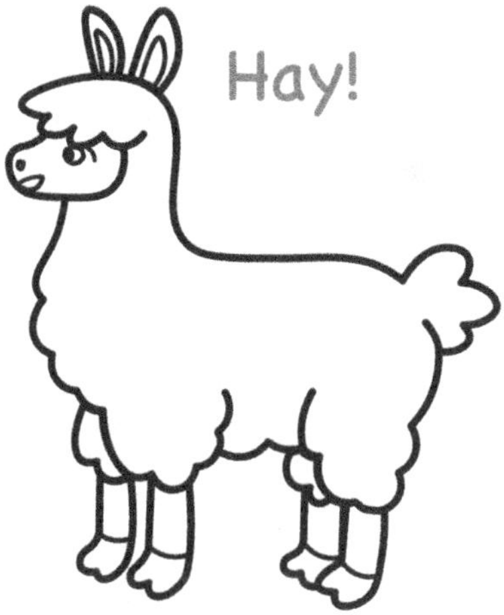

Hay!

How did the little trees sleep at camp?

Like a log!

What do hikers do if they forget their eating utencils?

They take a fork in the road!

Knock, knock.

Who's there?

Wooden.

Wooden who?

Wooden eat the fish sticks if I were you!

Knock, knock.

Who's there?

Wanda.

Wanda who?

Wanda start a food fight?!

Knock, knock.

Who's there?

Slime.

Slime who?

Slime-a beans for lunch again!

Knock, knock.

Who's there?

Ooze.

Ooze who?

Ooze going to tell the Chef that we don't like this food!

Knock, knock.

Who's there?

Waffle.

Waffle who?

Waffle you think is for breakfast?

Knock, knock.

Who's there?

Earl.

Earl who?

Earl be happy when the care package from home comes in the mail!

Knock, knock.

Who's there?

Lion.

Lion who?

Still lion in my sleeping bag!

Knock, knock.

Who's there?

Venice.

Venice who?

Venice it time to make s'mores!

Knock, knock.

Who's there?

Fangs.

Fangs who?

Fangs for taking that snake out of my tent!

Knock, knock.

Who's there?

Ewe.

Ewe who?

Ewe are up the creek without a paddle!

Knock, knock.

Who's there?

Ester.

Ester who?

Ester time for a ghost story?!

Knock, knock.

Who's there?

RV.

RV. who?

RV ever going to stop telling jokes?!

Knock, knock.

Who's there?

Bats.

Bats who?

Bats all folks!

Also Available from Howling Moon Books

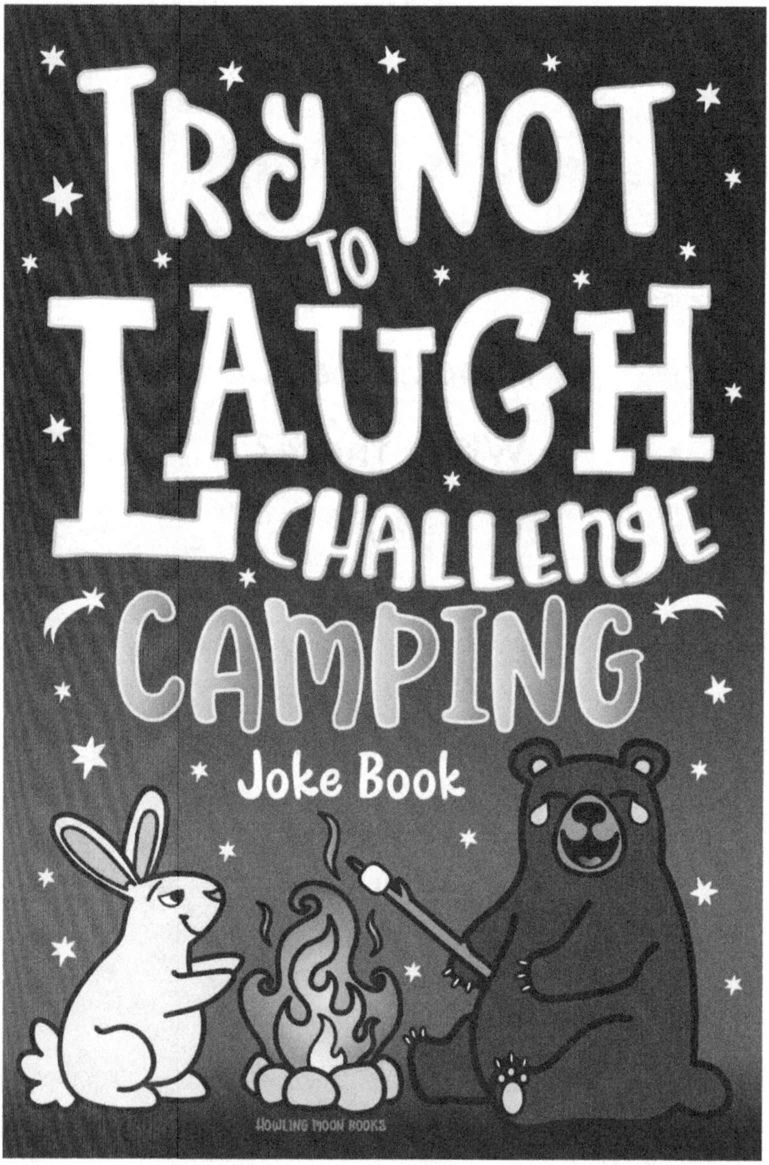

We hope that summer camp was filled with more hoots, howls, & chuckles with these campfire funnies!

Help us Spread the Laughter!

We want S'more Campers to LOL on their next outdoor adventure!

Please consider leaving us a review on Amazon.com. We value your feedback & greatly appreciate your time!

Thank you!

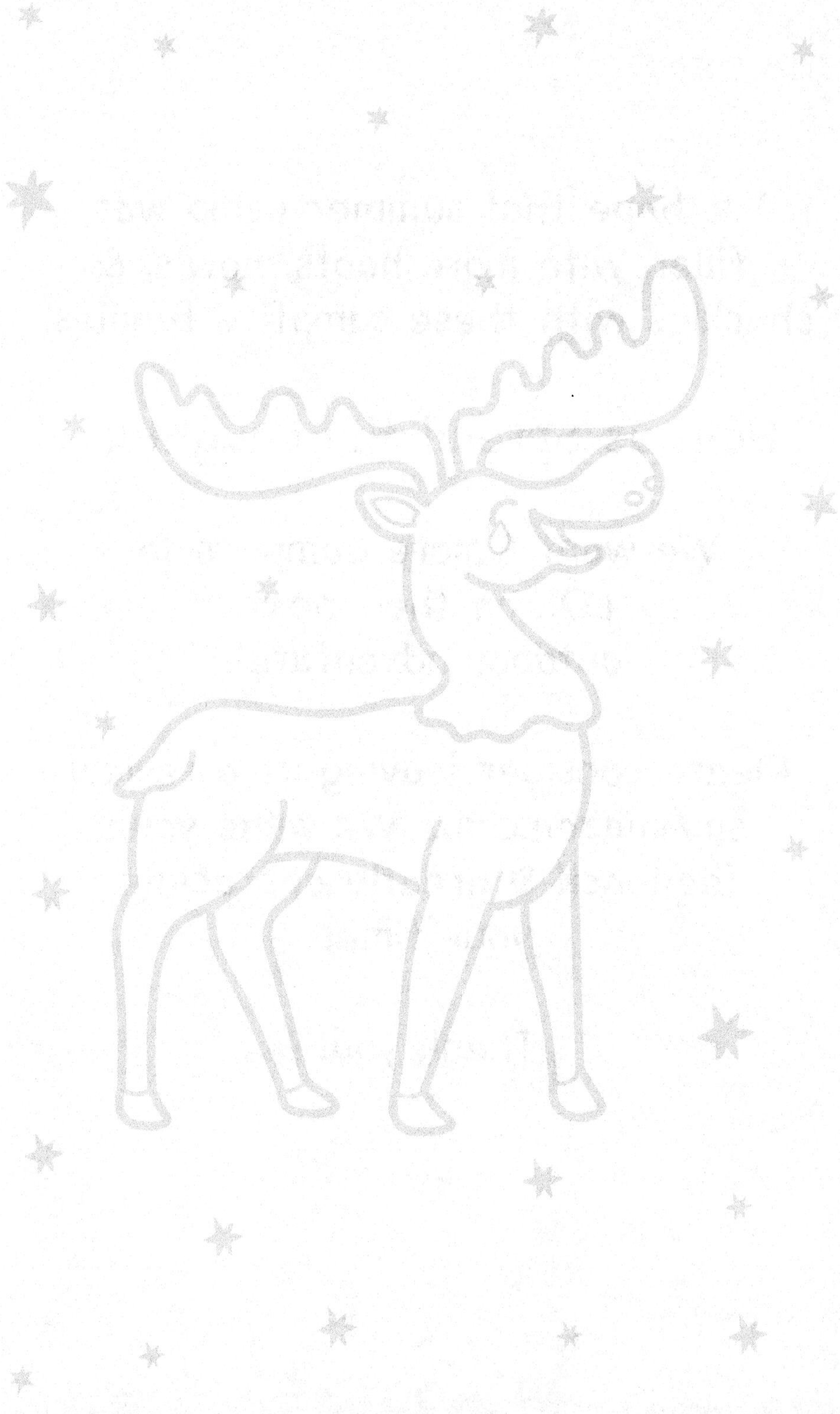

Also Available from Howling Moon Books

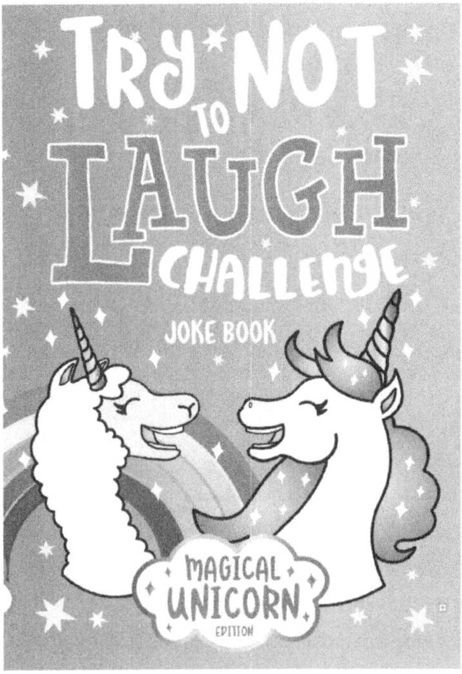

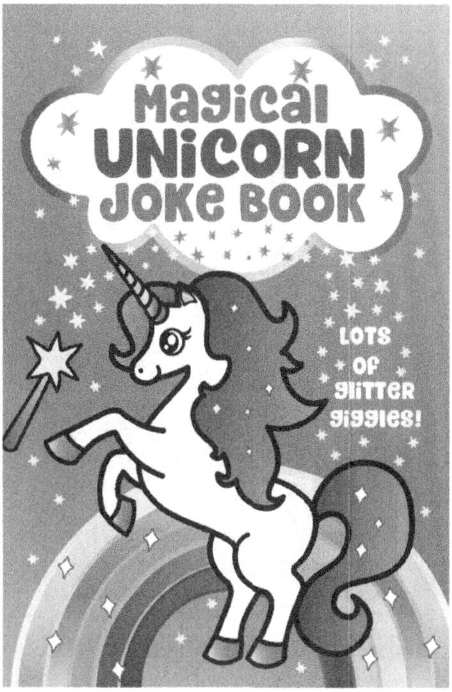

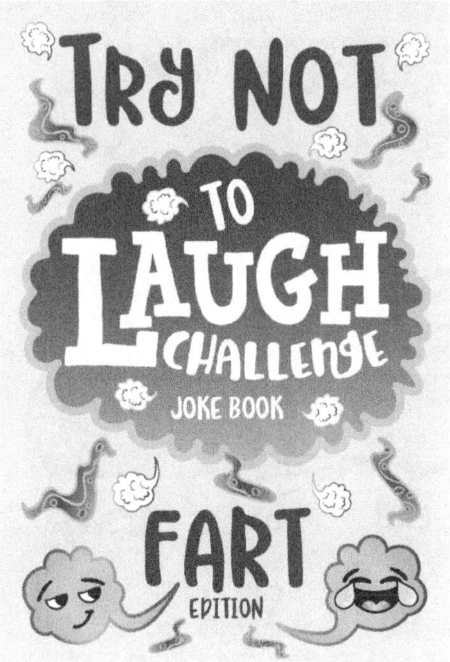

Also Available from Howling Moon Books

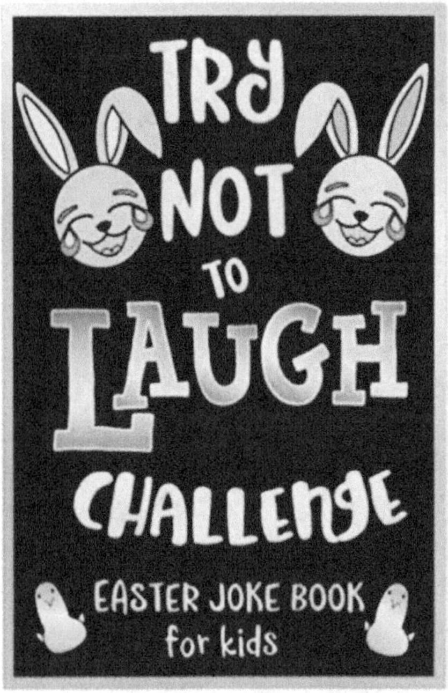

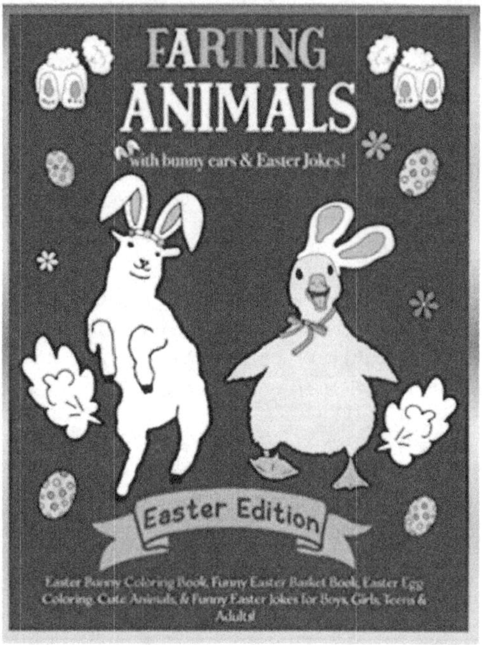

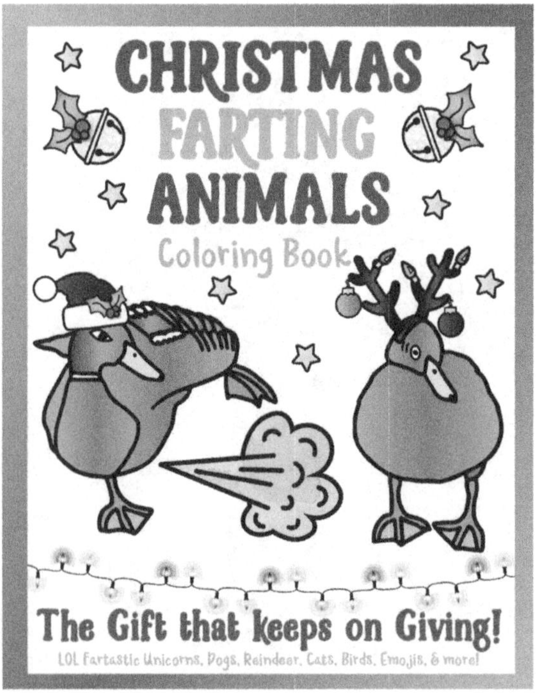

Also Available from Howling Moon Books

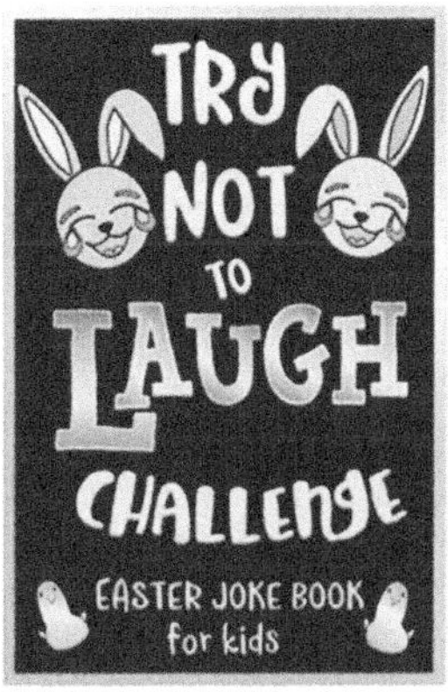

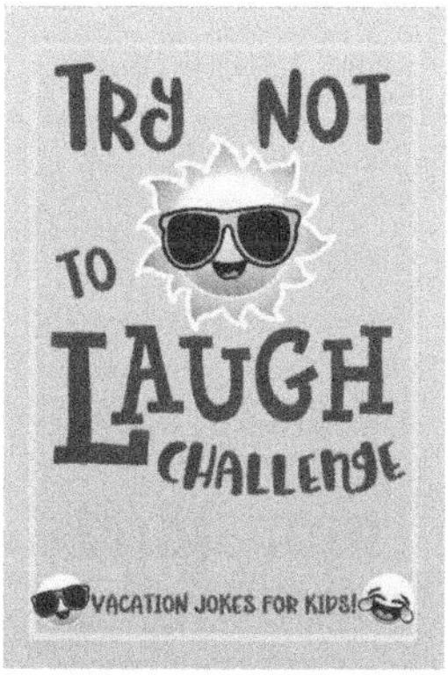

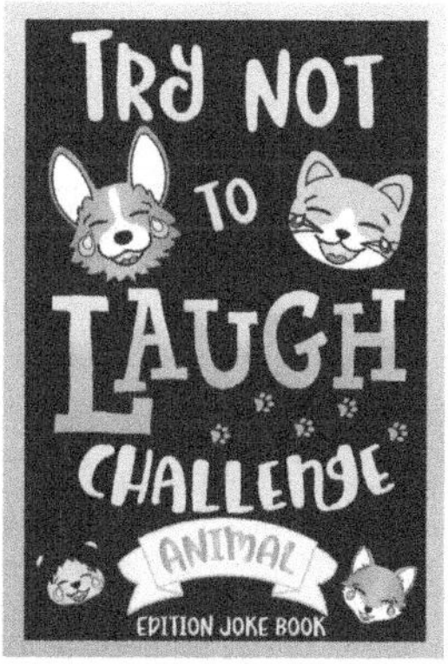

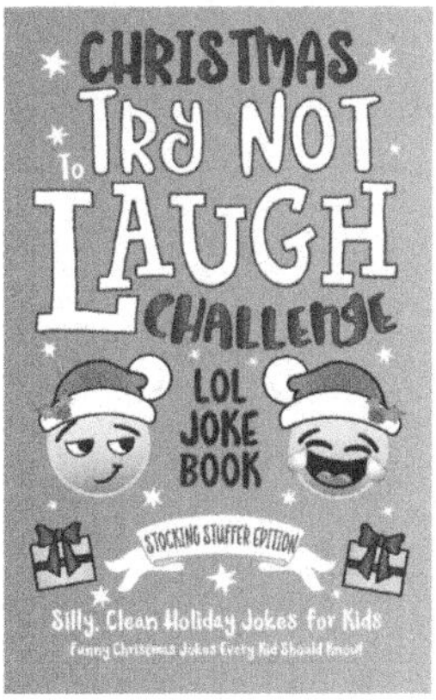

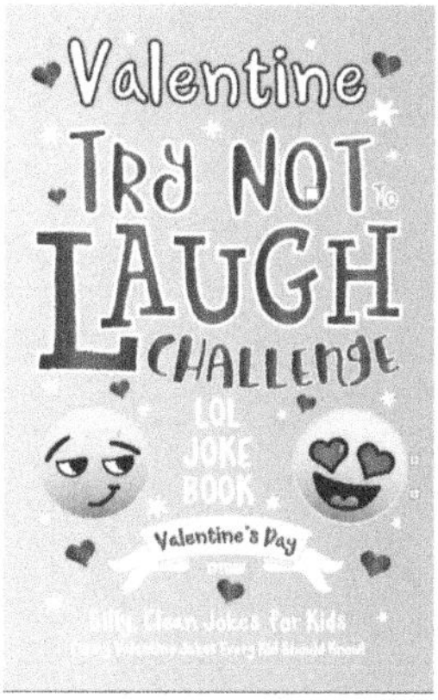

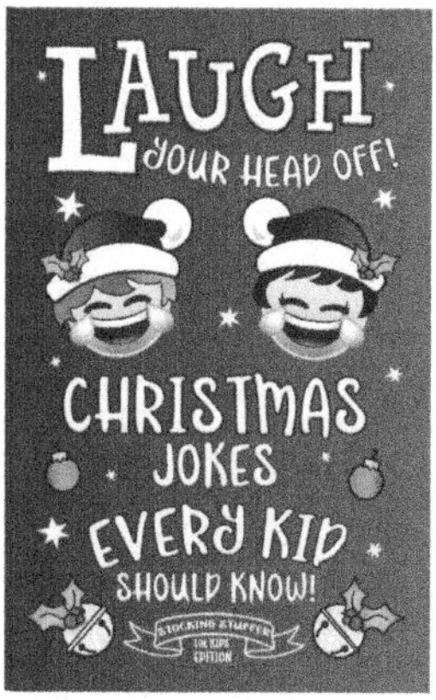

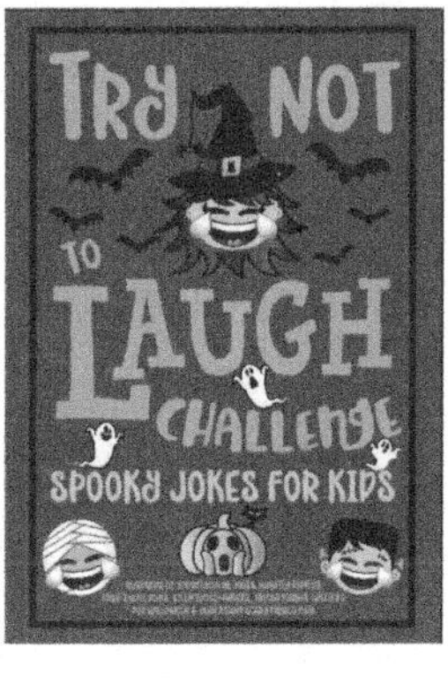

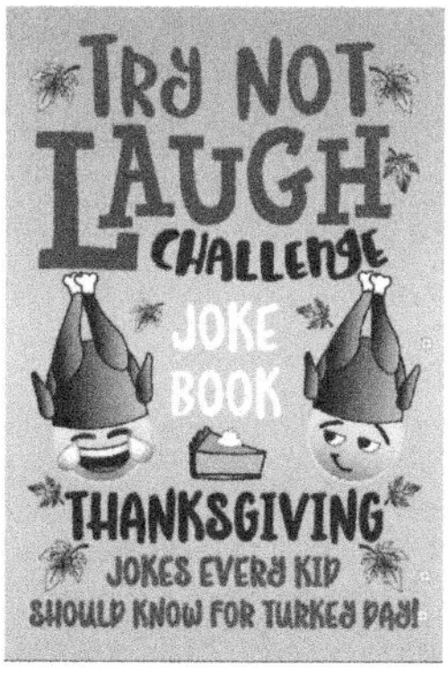

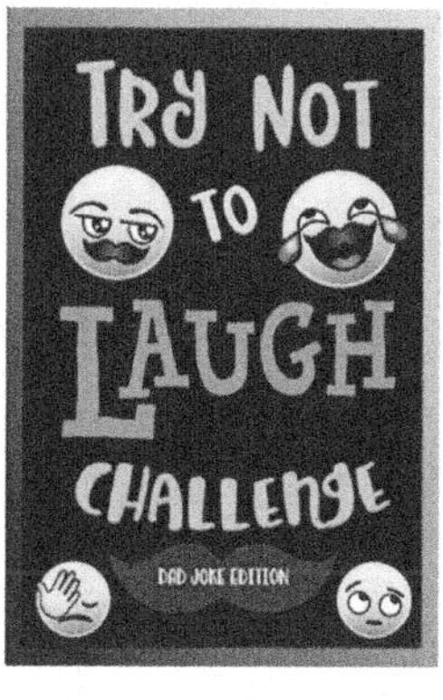